mark mattock
roses
for the smaller garden

Quadrille

Editorial Director: Jane O'Shea

Creative Director: Mary Evans

Project Editor: Carole McGlynn

Art Editor: Rachel Gibson

Production: Vincent Smith, Nancy Roberts

Picture Research: Nicola Phoenix

Editorial Assistant: Katie Ginn

First published in 2001 by Quadrille Publishing Limited

Alhambra House

27–31 Charing Cross Road

London WC2H OLS

This paperback edition first published in 2002

Cataloguing-in-Publication Data: a catalogue record for this book is
available from the British Library.

ISBN 1 903845 99 8

Printed and bound in Germany

Contents

the rose story

The rose is one of the oldest flowering plants known to man and one of the most enduring and universal in its appeal. Although native to the northern hemisphere, roses are now grown in most countries of the world, including those in the southern hemisphere. Many books have been written about the history and legends of roses and all rosarians have fascinating stories to relate. The interest of this book, however, lies in the practical application of the knowledge achieved by the great gardeners and rose breeders of the past and, in particular, in the selection of types and varieties of rose for the modern gardener faced with limited space. It is fascinating to trace the process by which roses have evolved from their wild origins, first through gradual mutation and adaptation over the centuries and, more recently, through the ingenuity displayed by rose breeders in the techniques of hybridization to produce roses that meet the needs of today's small gardens.

Early history

Since before the beginnings of written history the rose has featured in stories of adventure. Even before the formation of the great civilizations of the Near and Middle East, travellers were bringing specimens of this wondrous plant back from the East. Army mercenaries often included roses in their war booty, to grace the gardens of their masters.

We know the Ancient Greeks cultivated roses. Coins from Rhodes, dating from 500B.C., are imprinted with an image of a single, open flower, understood to be the rose. Theophrastus (c.370–c.286B.C.), in his classification of all known plants of the time, writes of a rose having up to one hundred petals, thought to refer to *Rosa centifolia*, and of the five-petalled briar rose, still to be found today.

By the time of the Roman civilization, roses had become a symbol of wealth and luxury. Early Romans grew roses in specially constructed houses, heated to produce blooms during the winter. Roses were often used in the garlands presented to military heroes and their petals strewn over the floors of banqueting halls. The ruins of Herculaneum and Pompeii left after the catastrophic volcanic eruption of Vesuvius in A.D.79 show villas surrounded by 'peristyle' gardens of restricted size, very like our smaller gardens today. Boundary walls provided privacy from other buildings and central pools were often surrounded by flower beds in which roses would have grown, among other popular flowers. Roses are also depicted in frescoes found at Pompeii.

Pliny's *Natural History* features references to roses that are thought to be forms of what we can now identify as *R. alba, R. canina, R. centifolia, R. damascena* and *R. gallica*. But after the fall of the Roman Empire few, if any, references to these roses appeared in literature until King Childebert of France presented a rose garden to his queen in A.D.550, though we know that roses were cultivated in the Byzantine Empire and Persia. Emperor Charlemagne is also credited with growing roses in his gardens. But from the first century A.D., roses that survived in the West did so in the gardens of monasteries and large houses throughout Europe.

Religion and commerce had a great influence on what the poet Sappho called 'the queen of flowers'. The distribution of roses through the Mediterranean countries of southern and western Europe roughly parallels the spread of Islam, reaching Spain in the eighth century. And the use of rosewater in medicine (to mask the unpleasant smell of the potions used), as well as rose oil in perfume and cosmetics, and rose-leaf tea as a herbal drink, ensured that records of its survival appeared throughout the Middle Ages. During the twelfth and thirteenth centuries the Crusaders introduced Europe to the varieties cultivated in Asia when they brought back specimens from the Holy Land. Among those mentioned is *R. gallica* var. *officinalis*, referred to as 'the apothecary's rose' for its prominence in medicinal use as rosewater.

By the early seventeenth century a number of different species and naturally occurring varieties or sports were being described in printed Herbals, both in England and elsewhere in Europe. Most of these fell into the groups known as Gallicas, Damasks and Albas, with their many-petalled, rosette-shaped blooms and shrubby growth. Some time later, another, similar group – the fragrant Centifolias – was developed by French and Dutch nurserymen, who had begun to sow seed and select the best seedlings to develop as new varieties. At around the same time, the European settlement of the New World introduced roses cultivated in Europe to North and South America and the settlers sent back to Europe indigenous American species, including *Rosa virginiana* and *Rosa californica*. As far as we can tell, up to the eighteenth century roses grown in gardens would have been planted in beds, trained against walls and fences and mixed with other plants – never allowed to predominate.

▶ *Rosa gallica var. officinalis, 'the apothecary's rose', was reputedly introduced by crusader Thibault IV to Provins in the Champagne district of France in the Middle Ages. The area became the commercial source of this medicinal rose, remaining so for six centuries.*

One of the earliest examples of a garden planned for roses was at the palace of Malmaison, in Paris, created in 1799 for Napoleon's wife, later the Empress Josephine, to indulge her passion for roses. Her rosarian gardener, André Dupont, sowed seed from hips to make selections for new varieties. By the time of Josephine's death in 1814, the collection at Malmaison contained over 250 varieties of rose planted in narrow beds, with paths running down both sides, allowing all blooms to be examined at close quarters. Many varieties were recorded with remarkable accuracy and delicacy by the great court painter, Pierre-Joseph Redouté. A number of his subjects can still be found in gardens today, though the size of the bushes and their limited season of bloom makes them unsuitable for the small contemporary garden.

The appearance of China roses

China roses, meanwhile, having reached southern Europe via the Silk Route (the trading route from the East through the Middle East to southern Europe), spread to northern Europe around the 1750s. We know that a clone of *Rosa x odorata* was grown at the Botanic Gardens at Kew in 1769 and *Rosa chinensis* var. *semperflorens* (Slater's Crimson China) arrived in Europe at this time. The remarkable characteristic of China roses, more sparse in growth than European roses, was their ability to repeat flower through the summer, which transformed the development of roses in Europe after the 1780s. The China rose was not hard to propagate and within a short time we find it recorded in France, Britain and the United States.

The brothers Louis and Philippe Noisette, nurserymen in Paris, France and Charleston, South Carolina, assisted in the dissemination of the China rose. A wealthy rice planter, John Champney of Charleston, produced a hybrid between it and *Rosa moschata,* which he named Champney's Pink Cluster. Seeds of this were gathered by Philippe Noisette and from the plants he raised, he selected a white rose to send to his

◀ Rosa *Adelaïde d'Orléans, a* R. *sempervirens hybrid dating from 1826, is a typical once-flowering Rambler that is still grown today (colour engraving by Victor from a painting by Redouté).*

brother Louis in Paris. This is recognized to be the first of the Noisette roses referred to by Redouté as *Rosa noisettiana.* Among its direct descendants we still grow the fragrant climbers, Gloire de Dijon and Madame Alfred Carrière.

The tea-scented China roses were not hardy enough to be planted outdoors in northern climates, so during the nineteenth century they were grown in conservatories and crossed with hardier outdoor types like Hybrid Perpetuals, the first of the Modern roses. Not only did the Hybrid Perpetuals have upright growth and pointed buds, but many varieties were crimson, a colour absent in roses to date. This led eventually to the production of 'Hybrid Teas'.

In France the China rose had taken another direction and been developed into a group known as Tea-scented China roses, either for the resemblance of their scent to fresh tea leaves or because they were imported from the East in tea chests. The Tea roses share many characteristics with the China roses, being delicate in their growth and subject to frost in northern climates. Their lovely, dainty blooms often had pointed buds and they were repeat flowering. Bourbon roses such as Madame Pierre Oger and Zéphirine Drouhin, the thornless rose, as well as Portland roses, all owe their existence to the Tea-scented China rose.

It was not until the mid-1800s that the legacy of early interest in the rose came to full fruition. The plantsmen of Victorian England were the first to carry out hybridization on any scale and, later in the century, breeding programmes in Europe and elsewhere developed the rose further, the exact directions being determined by the taste of the day and the public's shifting perceptions of rose beauty. At this time roses were bred almost entirely for their individual blooms (this was the age of the exhibition flower), with no regard for the plant's habit. But the first Hybrid Teas constituted a new kind of rose: short and upright growing, with high-pointed buds and flowers and large, glossy leaves – and they flowered repeatedly. Their habit of growth influenced the way roses started to be grown in gardens, in isolated 'rose beds'. This made sense aesthetically and practically since they all needed similar culture, flowered at the same time and were hard to mix attractively with other plants.

The evolution of modern roses

A feature of the development of domestic architecture world-wide since 1900 has been the advent of the smaller garden. Now that most houses, especially in towns, are small and compact, each has its own modest garden space or yard. Since we like to enhance our immediate surroundings with flowering plants, it is no surprise to find the rose in one of its forms decorating our confined outdoor living areas.

As the style and proportions of our gardens have been modified, so has the rose. By the early 1900s, when bedding roses included a few Hybrid Perpetuals and the early Hybrid Teas, purists in both the Old and the New Worlds still believed roses should be strictly segregated in beds, mixed plantings being reserved for the cottage garden. So in the large town or country-house gardens of the Establishment, pride of place in the centre of sweeping lawns was given over to formal rose beds, the same rose varieties grown and trained as standards being the only intrusions permitted.

The upright Hybrid Teas, with their pointed blooms, soon became so popular that they almost obliterated the Old roses with their cupped blooms and bushy growth. The Hybrid Tea was subsequently slimmed down, making it appropriate for smaller gardens. The colour range was also expanded from the pinks, purples and whites which had existed before. In 1910 the first of the yellow roses appeared and, from these introductions, a whole range of warmer colours.

During the 1930s the Hybrid Tea was further refined to exaggerate its scrolled bud and pointed bloom. A milestone in its development was the introduction of the extraordinary variety known as Peace. In the immediate pre-war years its appearance on the trial beds of its raisers, Antoine and François Meilland in the south of France, excited much admiration. In addition to its large blooms and superb foliage, it had a vigour unheard of in a Bush rose. Propagating material

The hundred-petalled rose, Rosa centifolia, *was first referred to by Theophrastus, the 'father of botany', around 300*B.C. *(painting by Redouté).*

was sent off to the raisers' distributors in Germany, Italy and the United States so it could be offered to a wider public. But war intervened and before long Peace had appeared under the name of Gioia in Italy, Gloria Dei in Germany and in France, the country of its origin, as Madame A. Meilland. At the end of the hostilities in 1945, with the inauguration of the United Nations, the wonder rose was officially launched under its most appropriate and universal name – Peace.

Alongside the development of Hybrid Teas, the Polyantha roses (grown previously in pots in conservatories) attracted the interest of rose breeders who developed them into the Polyantha pom-poms. Resilient and hardy, with clusters of small Rambler-like flowers, they became the most fashionable bedding roses of the day. In the mid-1920s, Svend Poulsen, the master Danish rose hybridizer, crossed the Polyantha pom-pom with the Hybrid Tea, to produce a cluster-flowered rose with larger blooms. His dream of creating a new breed of bedding roses came to fruition in the 1930s with the release of his new varieties of 'Poulsen rose', which he named after his daughters Ann, Kirsten, Karen and Else. Once they began arriving from other sources, these roses were known as 'Hybrid Polyanthas' and international rose breeders developed their blooms to resemble those of the Hybrid Teas more closely. By the 1950s, with the introduction of such great varieties as Fashion and Spartan from the United States, these roses differed so much from the earlier varieties that the new term, Floribunda, was universally adopted.

Hybrid Tea and Floribunda roses continued for a time to be regarded in the traditional way, as single-planting subjects. But the rise of the garden centre in the United States and its spread to Europe in the 1960s tempted gardeners to try mixing bedding roses with the herbaceous plants suddenly available in containers. As a result, today's gardeners regard beds, borders and containers as suitable arenas for roses.

Today's following for miniature roses started with *Rosa roulettii*, a tiny shrub 5cm/2in high, discovered in 1818 by Dr Roulet, growing in pots on window sills in a Swiss village.

But it was not introduced commercially until 1922 and from such beginnings came a whole industry dealing with these tiny plants and their descendants; by 1977, there were more than 325 Miniature roses. Twenty or so years later, the miniaturized 'patio' rose was introduced in Great Britain specifically for small gardens, as a result of breeding the shorter-growing Floribundas.

Climbing roses

Climbing roses have evolved too. Until the middle of the last century most Climbers were the result of mutations of current varieties of bedding rose, for example Climbing Crimson Glory. These, along with Ramblers like the famous Dorothy Perkins, a lax-growing type of Climber bred in 1901 by the large U.S. firm of Jackson Perkins, were midsummer flowering only; they spent the rest of the season producing new growth on which to flower the following year. But at almost the time of the Floribunda's emergence, in the middle of the twentieth century, Climbers with repeat-flowering characteristics started to be introduced. The first was the well-known variety, New Dawn, which has influenced the breeding of repeat-flowering Climbers ever since. It is reputed to be a mutation of the tall, non-recurrent Rambler, Dr W. Van Fleet, resembling this rose in all respects other than its flowering time.

Since the late 1980s, a new type of Climbing rose, known as the 'patio climber' or climbing Miniature, has been bred for the gardener faced with the vertical aspect of boundaries in the small garden. Their foliage and blooms are in perfect scale with the plant's size – they are miniature-flowered as well as having small leaves and being short – and the blooms are borne in profusion from top to toe. The first, growing to 2m/6ft tall and 1m/3ft wide, was the bright, golden-yellow Laura Ford. They proved excellent subjects for confined spaces, from fences to pillars.

Shrub roses

Modern Shrub and Hybrid Musk roses, with ideal repeat-flowering characteristics, were developed in the twentieth century for the modern garden, where they may be used in mixed plantings or even hedges. Hybrid Musks bear large sprays of double flowers on tall, graceful growth, resembling a refined Floribunda. The best varieties were bred between 1900 and 1930 by the Reverend Pemberton of Essex, England. Modern Shrub roses are the result of crossing Hybrid Teas and Floribundas with a wide variety of different Species roses to produce a diverse class of Shrub roses with robust growth and flowers of modern appearance. The best-known of these is the group developed in England by David Austin and known as English roses.

With the arrival of the successful Hybrid Tea roses in the early twentieth century, many of the Old rose varieties simply disappeared and few were offered in growers' catalogues. However, in a concerted effort led by rosarian Graham Stuart Thomas, collectors searched out and preserved surviving examples of Old roses in their gardens. This revival of interest led eventually to their being exported around the world, from about 1950 onwards. The new English roses, introduced in the 1970s, combine the charms of these Old Garden roses with the merits of modern hybrids – full, many-petalled blooms, contemporary colours, glorious fragrances and, in many cases, disease resistance and a neat growing habit. With their more natural, informal appearance, they are well suited to mixed borders.

Meanwhile, the popularity of the shrubby growth and free flowering of the Floribundas coupled with the demand for a ground-hugging plant to suppress annual weeds influenced the more recent introduction of a selection of spreading (Ground Cover) roses, the so-called Bodendecker roses, originating in Germany. These not only make excellent ground-cover plants but are also suitable for growing in containers. They evolved from *Rosa wichurana*, a Species that is semi-prostrate in habit, so they hug the ground, yet they have a strong affinity to Floribundas, with blooms down to ground level. They are usually marketed under the popular County and Flower Carpet series.

▸ Striped Rosa Mundi *started life as a sport of* Rosa gallica var. officinalis (R. gallica 'Versicolor') *and it was possible to find both forms of bloom on the same plant, flowering simultaneously.*

Classification of roses

There are of course hundreds of roses, all of which deserve much more space than we can allot either in this book or in the garden. However, their influence is important in the development of our Modern Garden roses and the definition of rose types which follows is the result of much deliberation by the World Federation of Rose Societies to clarify what may seem to be a bewildering family.

Modern Garden roses

These refer to roses of hybrid origin that bear no strong resemblance to wild (Species) roses and were not included in any classification in general use before the introduction of Hybrid Tea roses. Within this group are Non-climbing and Climbing types.

Non-climbing Modern Garden roses

Plants with self-supporting stems. These roses are sub-divided into recurrent-flowering roses, whose flowering season is long or with a marked resurgence later, and non-recurrent flowering roses, whose flowering season is limited to spring or summer with, at best, only occasional blooms in the autumn. By far the bigger group are the non-climbing, recurrent-flowering roses, which are divided into the following categories:

Shrub roses are defined as plants that are usually taller and/or possibly wider than Bush roses and are particularly suitable for use as specimen plants. Ground Cover roses fall within this category.

Bush roses are varieties of moderate height that are particularly suitable for cultivation in groups.

Hybrid Tea roses usually have flowers of medium to large size; the petals of double and semi-double varieties overlap to form a conical, ovoid or other symmetrical centre and those of single varieties are large and form a shapely bud. They lend themselves to being cut as individual flowers (with or without side buds) on a long stem.

Floribunda roses are distinguished primarily by a mass of flowers produced in trusses, clusters or on many stems. They may be single, semi-double or double.

Polyantha roses have small double flowers, usually of rosette form, borne in large clusters, and distinctive foliage, the leaflets being smaller than those of Floribunda roses.

Miniature roses have miniature flowers, foliage and growth.

Climbing Modern Garden roses

These are defined as climbing or rambling plants with long sprawling or arching stems requiring support. Again they are sub-divided into non-recurrent flowering Climbing roses, whose flowering season is limited to spring or summer with, at best, only occasional blooms in the autumn, and recurrent-flowering Climbing roses, whose flowering season is long or with a marked resurgence later. Within both groups of Climbing rose are:

Ramblers, climbing roses with lax stems.

Climbers, with stiffer stems than Ramblers.

Climbing Miniatures or patio climbers, with very small flowers and foliage.

Each ultimate class may be further divided into double (normally having more than 20 petals), semi-double (8–20 petals) and single flowered (fewer than 8 petals).

Old Garden roses

This refers to roses that were already well established in classifications in common use before the introduction of Hybrid Tea roses. These classes were based largely on presumed genetic and botanical affinities and, in general, do not fit into the modern classification based mainly on garden use. Again, they are divided into Non-climbing and Climbing types.

Non-climbing Old Garden roses

have self-supporting stems and include the following types:

Alba Roses displaying the influence of *Rosa alba*.

Bourbon Roses displaying the influence of *Rosa x bourboniana*, supposedly a hybrid between the China rose and Autumn Damask.

Boursault Roses supposedly displaying the influence of *Rosa chinensis* and *Rosa pendulina*.

China Roses displaying the influence of *Rosa chinensis*.

Damask Roses displaying the influence of *Rosa damascena*.

Gallica Roses displaying the influence of *Rosa gallica*.

Hybrid perpetual Roses usually inter-breeding Bourbon roses with China or Damask roses.

Moss Roses with mossy outgrowth on sepals and/or pedicels.

Portland Roses allied to Duchess of Portland (a hybrid), suggesting the influence of China and Damask Roses.

Provence (centifolia) Roses displaying the influence of *Rosa centifolia*.

Sweet briar Roses displaying the influence of *Rosa eglanteria* (syn. *R. rubiginosa*).

Tea roses Roses displaying the influence of *Rosa x odorata*, supposedly a hybrid between *Rosa chinensis* and *Rosa gigantea*.

Climbing Old Garden roses

are climbing or rambling plants with long sprawling or arching stems normally requiring support. They divide as follows:

Ayrshire Roses displaying the influence of *Rosa arvensis*.

Boursault Roses supposedly displaying the influence of *Rosa chinensis* and *Rosa pendulina*.

Climbing Tea Climbing roses with flowers similar to those of Tea roses.

Noisette Roses displaying the influence of *Rosa x noisettiana*, supposedly a hybrid between *Rosa chinensis* and *Rosa moschata*.

Sempervirens Roses displaying the influence of *Rosa sempervirens*.

Wild roses

These include Species roses and their varieties or hybrids (either single- or double-flowered) which bear a strong resemblance to the species. They are divided into Non-climbing and Climbing types, defined as before.

roses in the small garden

Roses are among the easiest, and most amenable, plants to grow. After good feeding and reasonable care and attention, they will thrive in almost any soil and give years of enjoyment. No matter how small your garden, or how irregular the boundaries, whether you are hemmed in by walls, fences or hedges, there is a rose for every aspect, bringing colour throughout the summer months. If you have an awkward corner, a Shrub rose will bring interest to it and if you wish to add height to a flower bed, a standard rose could be the solution. Climbing roses provide vertical decoration at and above eye level, while some of the old Ramblers, no longer planted on walls and fences because their flowering season is so short, may be grown to twine through old trees.

Choosing roses for your garden

▲ *Climbing rose Compassion, trained on a dividing trellis and flowering profusely, frames the picture presented by the geometric shapes of the clipped box and the mixed border featuring the Floribunda, Iceberg, a reliable old favourite.*

Whether you are thinking about planting a single specimen rose or a quantity to group together, you need to be sure that you have chosen correctly. First ask yourself some pertinent questions about what you want the rose(s) to do.

Is it to grow against a wall or fence? Which direction will it face? If your rose is to face a northerly or easterly aspect, it will be in shade for a greater part of the day, so you will need to select a free-flowering variety, like pale pink Compassion or champagne-coloured Penny Lane, which bloom well even in shade. What colour flowers do you prefer? You know what your favourite colour is, but will this be the right colour to plant against a brick or stone wall or a painted wooden fence? Will it complement companion plants or, if container grown, the terracotta colour of clay pots? Where roses are grown on a terrace or patio adjacent to the house you may also want to bear in mind the colour scheme of the living area or even of the curtains that frame it when viewed through the windows. How big is the wall to be covered? You will need to look up the plant's mature height and, for a high wall, choose a tall-growing variety such as Summer Wine or Madame Alfred Carrière.

Is the rose to plant in a mixed border or an island bed? How will you choose between large-flowered (Hybrid Tea) roses, cluster-flowered roses (Floribundas), both upright-growing, or bushy Shrub roses? What colour are the plants next to the rose? How tall need it grow to fit into the overall 'picture'? It is important to find out the mature height of your proposed planting and never a good idea to plant a tall, leggy variety at the edge of a much used path, though it could have a role at the back of a border. The same of course applies to the spread of a broad shrub, as you do not want to have to brush against soggy foliage in wet weather. But in the middle of a bed Shrub roses such as Charles Notcutt or Ballerina could look good. Do you want to be able to cut blooms for indoors? If so what is the colour scheme of your furnishings? The best roses for cutting are long, smooth-stemmed varieties.

Roses are excellent subjects to grow alongside other garden plants, and it is important to exploit the potential of mixing different flower shapes and textures. Suitable companions are discussed in more detail later in the chapter (see page 46). Having decided on the type of rose, the colour of its bloom and foliage and the overall size of the plant, it is now time to begin the enjoyable task of selecting the exact variety, or varieties, for your garden.

Selecting for confined spaces

In a small area any plant must pay its rent by giving good returns for the space allotted to it and this is particularly true of roses. It is very easy to look at pictures of beautiful roses and to make up your mind that you must have such

▼ *This mixed border on the boundary features a happy use of the Rambling rose Albéric Barbier, together with roses and other seasonal shrubs. Though Ramblers are not the best choice for small gardens, here it gives height where it is most needed.*

charmers as, say, Nevada or Frühlingsgold (both Shrub roses). The simplicity of their large, single open flowers can easily win you over, until you find that they will both grow to some 2.5m/8ft high and may dwarf anything else you wish to plant in your restricted border. Besides which, neither of them will give you the continuity of bloom that a smaller garden demands.

This does not mean, of course, that in a small garden you are destined to grow only the shorter Floribundas known as 'patio' roses. But you may wish to give preference to roses of a neat habit, with controlled vigour, that will not outgrow their allocated space. It also makes sense to select roses with good disease resistance as enclosed, urban sites are often airless and foster fungal growth such as mildew as well as attracting aphids. In terms of clothing walls and fences, you would generally choose Climbers or 'patio climbers' over Ramblers which have too lax and untidy a habit, in addition to flowering once only. Perhaps the most important quality is a long flowering time, or repeat flowering, because when not in flower roses may be of limited interest in the garden. Choosing roses that produce hips is another way of extending interest into the autumn; bear in mind that most of these are single- rather than double-flowered.

The more ornamental characteristics a rose has, the stronger its claim for inclusion in the smaller garden. A rose with attractive foliage as well as beautiful blooms will make more of a contribution when not in flower. Some Hybrid Tea roses, such as Royal William and Just Joey, have particularly attractive bronze-red juvenile foliage, while *Rosa glauca* (syn. *R. rubrifolia*) has glorious mauve-grey leaves which complement perfectly its single pink flowers and autumnal hips. Roses with good scent add an appealing quality to an

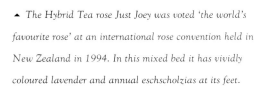

▲ *The Hybrid Tea rose Just Joey was voted 'the world's favourite rose' at an international rose convention held in New Zealand in 1994. In this mixed bed it has vividly coloured lavender and annual eschscholzias at its feet.*

individual's experience of a small garden, especially on a summer evening, as scents tend to be distilled in confined spaces. So, wherever possible, choose a fragrant rose over one that has no scent. There is no substance to the claims that 'modern roses have lost their smell'; writers in the 1880s were complaining about much the same thing and no doubt others will do so in the future, but contemporary rose breeders are all too conscious of retaining and enhancing this desirable characteristic whenever they can.

▲ *The apothecary's rose, Rosa gallica var. officinalis, can grow to 1.5m/5ft in height but in this narrow bed it is kept low by pruning out all the old wood immediately after blooming.*

◄ *Bourbon rose Zéphirine Drouhin is trained as a pillar to contrast with the white climbing rose, both of which add height to the beds on either side of the steps while helping to screen the unexceptional view beyond the garden.*

Purchasing your roses

Once you have chosen the roses you wish to plant it is important, first of all, to choose a good supplier. Talk to other gardeners and send off for mail-order catalogues because an informative catalogue can reveal much about the nursery. Most reputable suppliers give guarantees and offer a reliable service but it still makes sense to shop around. If you wish to see a particular rose variety 'in the flesh' before you consider buying it, you should visit local flower shows and open gardens as well as seeing what is on offer at your local garden centre or nursery.

Roses can be purchased in several different forms: what you choose will depend on availability and season.

Bare-rooted Nursery-fresh plants, dug from the rose fields where they have been grafted on to briar 'understocks', are sold either by mail order, or collected direct from the nursery in the traditional planting season, when the plants are in a dormant state during the winter months.

Containerized Having been propagated and grown in the nursery beds, these roses have been taken up and re-planted in pots so that they may be offered for sale in garden centres throughout the year. Some nurseries even prepare roses for sale by propagating them in pots on their own roots.

Pre-packed These roses, nursery grown, are lifted early in the season, sometimes before they are dormant, and sold in plastic packages, having been coated with wax preservative to enable them to withstand temperatures encountered inside the shops. Since many stores are kept too hot for the health of roses, it may be best to avoid this way of buying.

Rose awards

So universal is a love of the rose that almost all countries have a society devoted to its development and promotion. Most of these societies belong to The World Federation of Rose Societies, and all distribute their publications. One of their main activities is testing new varieties under local conditions, and rewarding the best with awards and recommendations. A study of roses receiving awards may make the choice of varieties easier. These awards are all listed in the book within the description of each profiled rose.

An explanation of the abbreviations used is given below:

AARS   All-American Rose Selection

ARS   American Rose Society

ADR   Anerkannte Deutsche Rose

HE   Harry Edland medal for best scented rose
        seedling of the year

PIT   President's International Trophy for best
        new seedling rose of the year

RNRS   Royal National Rose Society

TGC   Trial Ground Certificate

JMMM   James Mason Memorial Medal for a rose
        which has given pleasure to rose lovers
        (the actor was an enthusiastic grower).

▲ *The purple-grey foliage and hips of* Rosa glauca *can be used to great effect to enhance the colour of other flowering subjects. It is seen here with late summer-flowering shrubby mallow (*Lavatera 'Rosea'*).*

▸ *In this semi-formal design, symmetrically placed roses soften and embellish the layout. The soft colour of climbing rose* New Dawn *frames the view while Hybrid Musk roses flank the steps and pink Hybrid Teas furnish the beds.*

Planning rose beds and borders

The shape, size and position of beds and borders will to a great extent depend on the dimensions and layout of your garden as well as its style. Your layout might demand the open space of a lawn, with borders against the boundaries, backed by a wall or fence, or you may have a paved area in which island beds will find a setting. You may wish to create a formal look, with symmetrical borders containing a fairly regimented planting of neat, compact plants, or prefer the informality of an asymmetric bed which, through the careful placing of plants of different shapes, sizes and colours, has a balance of its own.

Planting an island bed

The term 'island bed' refers to a planted area in your garden which will be viewed from every side – a path, surrounding lawn or a paved area – so the planting has to look good all round. The idea of island beds started with formal beds cut out in geometric shapes in the lawns of nineteenth-century gardens. The more gardeners employed, the more intricate the shape of the bed could be: all the edging was laborious and time-consuming. If you are planning a new island bed, keep the outline simple – whether circular, elliptical, square or rectangular – to cut down the work involved. Its dimensions

will of course be governed by the site, but if you have the choice, make sure the relevant regular planting distances (see page 150) fit the bed exactly. Try not to make an island bed too deep or too wide because when working among the roses you will want to reach the middle of the bed without difficulty. If the bed has to be deep or wide, however, make access easier by laying carefully sited stepping-stones.

Besides keeping the edge of the lawn trimmed, nineteenth-century fashion also decreed that beds were edged with a low hedge, usually box (*Buxus sempervirens*) or lavender (*Lavandula*). These edged beds still exist in gardens of traditional formal design but new ideas have also developed out of them. We now see mixed beds, edged with modern 'patio' roses: Floribundas such as Festival, Mandarin or Queen Mother, or large Miniature roses of up to 45cm/18in in height, like Baby Masquerade or Royal Salute. The spreading Ground Cover rose varieties such as Avon or Kent are also used to edge beds. Using Ground Cover roses to fill awkward corners of an irregularly shaped island bed will help to prevent visitors or the postman taking a 'short cut' across an empty corner of the bed. When paths surround the island bed and an edging is not used, it is advisable to leave at least 45cm/18in between the front row of roses and the edge of the path. Avoid planting wide-spreading bedding varieties too near the edge as they would eventually overhang the path or lawn, causing the risk of clothing or lawn mowers being caught by a thorny branch.

The smaller your garden, the less likely you are to keep your island bed for bedding roses only. Low-growing spring-flowering plants, including bulbs, can be planted among roses to provide interest in another season. When planning the overall shape of your planting and looking for taller subjects, bear in mind that most of the Old Garden roses bloom for only a short midsummer season on the previous season's growth, and do not lend themselves to being restrained by pruning. However, Modern Shrub roses, including English roses, bloom on the current year's growth and may therefore be pruned to create the shape you want.

If you are mixing types of rose — for example, bedding roses such as Floribundas and Hybrid Teas with the more

▲ *Standard roses, with superb lavenders at their feet, have been planted closer together than normal and used in place of climbers to furnish a wall in this restrained, contemporary planting scheme.*

◀ *In an original twist on the idea of edging beds with low box hedges, this topiary feature cut into geometric shapes uses Rosa glauca as an attractive infill. The small blooms will be followed by a fine crop of brilliant red hips.*

vigorous Shrub roses – remember that they each require different planting distances and planting in well-ordered rows may be impossible. Include as many repeat-flowering roses as you can to ensure that the display is not limited to a few weeks in early summer. It is important to aim for an overall sense of balance when designing your planting, so bear this in mind when you mark out the planting positions. You may not wish to present an even bank of colour, in which case you should vary the selection of varieties to create clumps of different shape. Perfect balance can in any case be boring to the eye and an asymmetric design may bring more interest to your planting. For example, you may set the tallest 'focal point' plant deliberately off-centre to prevent a planting looking like a predictable and regimented pyramid.

When selecting subjects for island beds, make sure that what you choose is in proportion to the size and shape of the bed and any other plants you are using in the bed or in the background. You would not plant big Shrub roses in a small bed or even a small garden, however beautiful their blooms,

as they would be out of proportion. Standard roses and taller varieties can be included if you wish to 'lift' an otherwise flat bed, but they need careful siting (see page 34). As a general guideline, plant the low-growing 'patio' roses and Ground Cover roses at the front and the taller, more upright Hybrid Tea and Floribunda varieties in the middle of your island bed. Follow the planting distances on page 150 to ensure your selected roses will not obscure those growing behind them.

Roses in the mixed border

Most borders are intended to be seen from the front or sides, with paths, lawns or paved areas in front and, usually, a taller screen at the back. This screen, which may take the form of a wall, fence or hedge, will provide a background against which shorter subjects will be seen. Informality is easier to achieve in a border than an island bed. Many of today's mixed borders have evolved from the concept of the old herbaceous borders, which involved much work in weeding, dividing and re-planting perennials at regular intervals. Some still contain several of the old favourite clump-forming herbaceous perennials which make classic combinations with Shrub roses. Later in the chapter, subjects for planting alongside your roses are discussed in detail (see page 46).

In a rose border there is scope, provided the dimensions allow, to plant a host of different types of rose. Shapes, colours and sizes can be blended for an overall effect, or they may be deliberately contrasted for more impact. As we have seen, it is important to plan for interest through the seasons. Early flowering varieties such as Canary Bird, a fine yellow briar rose, could start the season. At 1.5m/5ft high, it is not too large for the smaller garden and its foliage is ornamental throughout the summer. Such a rose will provide a dainty companion to the splash of colour to follow, from the early summer-flowering Shrub roses, the summer and autumn repeat-flowering varieties of Floribunda and Hybrid Tea roses, as well as the patio and ground-hugging varieties, not forgetting the repeat-flowering Shrub roses which will carry your display through to autumn. If space allows, you could include some summer-flowering Species roses and hybrids which bear ornamental hips, like *Rosa* Geranium (a

▼ Demonstrating how roses of all types contribute to the mixed border, Shrub rose Charles de Mills and English rose Heritage with Hybrid Tea Silver Jubilee are greatly enhanced by the herbaceous perennials (below left).

▼ The Bourbon rose Zéphirine Drouhin can be grown as a freestanding shrub in a bed or as a Climbing rose to cover a wall (below right).

◀ *Modern Shrub rose Ballerina,*
seen here repeated through a bed
with gypsophila and violas,
offers a long season of interest.
Its apple-blossom pink blooms
continue until the first frosts,
after which it is smothered with
clusters of tiny bead-like hips.

moyesii selection), or one of the Rugosas or their hybrids, which will provide late autumn fruit and may show colour into winter if the birds leave the hips for your enjoyment.

How you arrange the different varieties depends on the effect you wish to achieve. For example, if room permits, Hybrid Musk roses such as Cornelia provide attractive arching shapes and look superb when surrounded, or fronted, by Ground Cover roses such as Avon, Berkshire or St. Tiggywinkle. A more upright variety like Kordes' Robusta will be well set off by a bushy Floribunda such as Anna Livia. If your border is backed by a wall, plant a Climbing rose against it for background interest – Compassion would complement Cornelia, Golden Showers would contrast effectively with Kordes' Robusta. If you do not have a fence or wall to support climbers, a planting of *Rosa moyesii* would provide taller tracery as background.

The size of the border will have a bearing on the shape you wish your roses to have when seen side-on from the house. The larger the border, the greater should be the size of the 'clumps' of roses used and repeating the clumps will create a sense of balance. When planting more than one of a variety, uneven numbers make the most amenable shape. Clumps of rose bushes help break up straight lines and escape the constraints imposed by rigidly defined boundaries, especially in long, narrow gardens. Use standard roses to provide extra height or give a broken line to the middle of a border, but if you wish to avoid the formality of a line of standards, grow shorter Climbing roses on pillars or obelisks to give the eye a vertical break. Choose a 'patio' or a more restrained Climber, such as Altissimo, Grand Hotel and Handel. Space once-flowering varieties among repeat-flowering subjects so whole areas are not left blank in autumn.

Using Shrub roses

When the Hybrid Teas and Floribunda roses heralded the arrival of the more manageable bedding roses, the previously popular once-flowering Shrub roses lost their importance in the smaller garden. But in recent years interest in these shrubby roses has grown, especially as Modern Shrub roses now have repeat-flowering bred into them. Some varieties may be used successfully as boundary hedges and garden dividers (see page 41), but there are other parts of the small, contemporary garden which cry out for the use of Shrub roses. From time to time roses have been introduced which defy classification but which, due to their appearance and habit of growth, have been marketed under the title of Modern Shrub roses. They are, in the main, repeat-flowering varieties which merely require trimming to size and shape each year.

Some of the Old Garden roses can be grown singly for their display in even the smallest border, although they have only a short flowering season. Moss rose Nuits de Young, deep purplish maroon, is smaller than the old favourite, Common Moss, and introduces a colour unusual in the modern garden. *Rosa gallica* 'Versicolor', better known as *Rosa mundi*, the striped rose of ancient times, is well worth the limited space it takes up; keep it in trim by removing the old flowering shoots each autumn. Many of the older hybrid Rugosas are too large for a confined space, but the variety Frau Dagmar Hastrup (see page 134), is more restrained in stature and is useful as a hedge or as a specimen plant in the mixed border. The same applies to the newer hybrid Rugosas from Germany, like Kordes' Robusta and The Compass rose. Other old favourites include Portland roses, such as De Rescht and Jacques Cartier, which combine the charm of Old Garden roses, too big for a limited space, with amenable size and the virtue of remontancy. When planting a Shrub rose, note its expected mature height. A short grower (up to 1m/3ft tall) needs less space around it than one of medium stature (see Planting Distances, page 150). Plant a group of a single variety closer than this, to grow into each other and eventually make a solid clump.

Rose breeders have made great strides in recent years. The idea of crossing some Old Garden roses with Modern Hybrid Teas and Floribundas originated with David Austin of Shropshire, England who named his brilliant selection 'English roses'. There are many excellent varieties to choose from, combining most of the outstanding characteristics of Old and Modern roses. The full, many-petalled blooms, soft colours and fragrance of the Old roses have been partnered by new colours, repeat-flowering and different styles of growth. If some are too tall to control as border plants, you could train them as pillar roses or grow them against a fence. The best varieties for this are Gertrude Jekyll (one of the best scented roses of all time), Graham Thomas and The Pilgrim.

Using Miniature and patio roses

A thriving pot rose industry has arisen in Europe in recent years. The important Danish rose breeding firm, Poulsen (of Hybrid Polyantha fame) is producing these pot roses by the million under the trade names of 'Parade' and 'Hit' roses, with such varieties as 'Pink Hit', 'Sun Hit' and 'Velvet Hit'. In the U.K. this has led to the development of a more robust-growing outdoor group, the 'patio' roses, greatly influenced by the cluster-flowered roses from which they were selected. These little bushes 45–50cm/18–20in high quickly became popular, especially for small gardens, where they can be planted in containers, making them ideal for use on terraces and patios, as well as at the front of small mixed borders.

▲ Patio roses such as Festival (voted Rose of the Year 1994) are selections from the shorter-growing Floribundas. They make ideal subjects for confined spaces, for edging beds and for growing in containers.

◀ Lax-growing Hybrid Musk roses, including Buff Beauty, with its soft colouring, make excellent subjects for the mixed border in conjunction with herbaceous perennials and other ornamental trees and shrubs.

Using Ground Cover roses

▲ The County Series are superb ground-hugging roses which bloom from early summer until the late autumn frosts. Kent (seen above left) has won many international awards and is ideal for small borders.

▲ Flower Carpet (above right) is a brilliant ground-covering rose. It was highly promoted throughout the world in the 1990s and is proving to be extremely disease-resistant.

Whatever the name given to these ground-hugging, sprawling shrubs, they offer great value when used in the small garden. The spreading habit of some of these lax-growing rose varieties still shows a strong affinity to *Rosa wichurana*, a trailing white scented species introduced from Japan in 1860 which gave rise to the range of Climbing roses known as the Ramblers. It was almost a century before their ground-hugging habit was used to advantage by breeders in the production of a new race of ground-covering roses. The Fairy, introduced in 1932, is the best known survivor of this early type and it has been much used in breeding since.

At the start of the latter half of the twentieth century two distinct types of ground-covering rose emerged and were quickly recognized for their worth by the landscaping sector of the horticultural industry. Big bushy plants arrived from The Netherlands, Denmark and France, while another wide-spreading, prostrate grower, typified by the Kordes' Gamebird series, came from Germany. These are the joint precursors of today's Ground Cover roses.

A decade or so after the appearance of these large, sprawling but unfortunately short-flowering varieties, exciting things began to happen. Through the use of the repeat-flowering, cluster-flowered (Floribunda) varieties in their breeding, low-growing, ground-hugging plants, often of only 1m/3ft across, were produced and introduced as Ground Cover roses. Planted about 1m/3ft apart, these sprawling bedding roses soon became popular for growing in both beds and borders, where they completely cover the ground, helping to suppress annual weeds. The attractive hummocks they produce are especially useful in small gardens, where they flower throughout the summer and autumn months until the winter's first frosts.

The need to differentiate these exciting modern roses from their sprawling forebears became clear as their many contemporary uses made themselves apparent. Marketing solved the problem. One selection, originating from varieties with common characteristics produced by the great hybridizers, Kordes in Germany and Poulsen in Denmark, was promoted in the U.K. under the 'family' name of The County Series, each variety named after a county in Britain. Other groups include the Flower Carpet series, originating in Germany, which has been successful worldwide. Much has

been written about the original vividly coloured variety, now called Pink Flower Carpet, especially of its disease-resistant foliage. White Flower Carpet (see page 123), my own favourite, is one of the best white scented bedding roses grown today. Other plant breeders too have been busy with this type of rose: Warner's Pathfinder is an eye-catching variety whose brilliant vermilion-scarlet blooms are borne in profusion on typical ground-hugging growth.

Besides the original use found for these roses, many were also budded on to stems to make attractive weeping standards (see page 34), especially those with abundant lax stems and good foliage, such as Avon, Gwent and Hertfordshire. Their ground-hugging characteristics can also be put to good use at the edge of a retaining wall, or close to the edge of a pool, where the plant's beauty will be reflected in the water. These ground-covering roses are also ideal in small beds, on banks, and as the edging for mixed shrub borders. Planted to within 60cm/2ft from the edge of a border, they will smother the soil surface and provide a perfect 'finish' to the bed.

▲ *The Fairy set standards by which more recent Ground Cover varieties are measured. The dainty sprays of tiny, soft pink double blooms are heaped layer upon graceful layer into a hummock-like shrub, seen here in a small bed with phlox and campanulas.*

Using standard roses

In Tenniel's famous illustrations for the children's classic, *Alice's Adventures in Wonderland*, the roses shown in the Queen of Hearts' garden are depicted as standards, that is, bush roses grafted on clear stems, bringing the blooms of even the shortest growers up to eye level. The varieties offered for sale as standards at nurseries and garden centres tend to be the most popular roses of a well-shaped, compact habit. They may be, but are not necessarily, large-flowered or even cluster-flowered varieties; patio roses, Shrub roses, and Ground Cover varieties may also be grown as standards to make simple accents in a garden. Avoid varieties which are tall, leggy or even straggly, because the resultant standard plant will be ungainly. Half-standard stems, used less often but in the same way, are usually 60cm/2ft tall and those of full standards are 1m/3ft.

Weeping standards are budded even higher, at 1.5m/5ft above ground level, and are another excellent means of adding height to a bed of uniformly growing bedding roses. The cascade of blooms hides the stake or ugly infrastructure. Budding the stem with a lax-growing variety produces a weeping standard; these are most attractive, though may need extra care and attention. Where Ramblers are used, remember that they are usually summer-flowering so, when pruning, leave the new growth to flower in the following year. You can remove older growth which has already flowered if this does not leave a gaping hole in the outline of the head. Some nurseries offer weeping standards of the prostrate-growing Ground Cover varieties which promise to be excellent additions to the small rose garden, blooming as they do for much longer than the old Ramblers. Often on quite short stems less than 1m/3ft in height, they are also an asset in a grouping of containerized plants, where these colourful small 'trees' provide a useful structural element. It is possible to train weeping standards over a metal frame, but I prefer the production of a natural weeping habit.

There is little difference in planting procedure between standard and Bush roses, except that the standards will need to be staked. Drive a stake into the ground to support the stem before planting a standard (to avoid damaging the roots), its top to come just below the lowest branches. Some

▲ *In this all-white planting, standard Iceberg roses are used to delineate and enhance the approach to this contemporary Australian home. Both the standards and the bedding Floribundas are underplanted with white impatiens.*

stems may be liable to produce suckers between the budding point and ground level. These are natural shoots from the briar understock which should not be left to mature. Remove by rubbing off the juvenile bud when it appears.

A good basic rule of planning and planting is to make sure the plant is in balance with its neighbours. Standard roses should not be too close to other standards (2–3m/6–9ft is a good distance), though the pairing or repetition of standards throughout a bed gives it a structural symmetry. Any underplanting should be in proportion, so use other roses which do not grow too tall, so you do not detract from

the focal effect of the standard. Do not plant standard roses in the path of an icy draught (from a gap in a wall, fence or hedge, for example); being higher makes them vulnerable to cold winds and in exposed areas protection may be needed.

When pruning standard Bush and Floribunda varieties, to ensure the new season's growth will produce an even, well-balanced shape, study the dormant growth buds and their position after pruning. Cut to an outward-pointing 'eye' so that new growth will not clog up the centre of the bushy head, allowing good air circulation. To avoid wind damage, cut longer shoots back by half before the winter.

Climbing roses on walls and fences

▲ *Fragrance fills the air and* *'walls' of colourful Climbing* *roses, among them New Dawn,* *surround and enclose this paved* *seating area at the far end of a* *small garden.*

In small town gardens with high boundaries, where there is often more space on walls than there is in the ground, Climbing roses are invaluable. They are as useful for covering unattractive close-boarded fences as boundary and house walls. There are many varieties of Climbing rose to choose from, to face all aspects and to cover all heights and situations. Before Modern roses arrived, Climbers were often used to clothe house walls, boundary walls and the dividing walls found within gardens as screens and windbreaks.

Climbing roses do not have a natural habit of climbing, being neither twining by nature nor having tendrils to support them, as do other climbers. They therefore need to be attached to a firm frame made by fixing taut wires or trellis to the support, be it a wall, fence or the house. If you want good wall coverage, it is important to train the basal shoots of Climbers out horizontally and to choose a variety that produces plenty of lateral shoots as well as being able to reach to the top of a fence. Good small-garden varieties with many lateral shoots include Compassion, Penny Lane, Summer Wine, New Dawn and Altissimo.

Bending the lower branches constricts the flow of sap, which ensures that foliage and flowers are generated from the base of the plant, whereas a Climbing rose trained vertically will often produce top growth only, leaving bare stems at eye level. Unless the lateral shoots are properly secured they can become quite unmanageable. Attach plastic-covered or galvanized wires to vine eyes or masonry nails screwed into the wall or fence; the wires should be strained tight and should stand about 5cm/2in proud of the wall to allow air circulation. The branches of the rose can then be attached by ties of soft brown twine rather than with wires or plastic string, which will eventually 'strangle' the shoots and therefore weaken the rose. When the strings disintegrate through age, they will simply need replacing with new ties. Wooden trellis panels, either attached to a wall or making a freestanding screen, can also be used as a support for Climbing roses. Fix the branches to the outside of the trellis so that it is easy to take the Climber down for pruning or retraining.

Not all varieties will be suitable for every situation which calls for a Climbing rose. Recommendations for which Climbers to grow where will be found on page 161. Many lists show varieties as being suitable for growing on shady northern aspects, which really means that they will tolerate the conditions experienced in such a situation. No rose likes to be grown in total shade, witnessed by the number of spindly, half-starved specimens seen struggling for existence in dark passages and other shady situations. But there may be a case for planting a Climber on a north-west facing wall or a favoured east-facing wall where it gets just enough sunlight to encourage blooms, especially if you choose the most free-flowering varieties. Climbing rose Mermaid is often recommended for walls in shade, but bear in mind that it may be suddenly cut to the ground by a harsh north-easterly wind. On the other hand, given some protection, Mermaid can reach enormous proportions, so you should remember this too, when searching for a favoured position for this variety of rose.

The most important criteria for even dappled shade would be the extraordinary freedom of bloom found in almost all of the recently bred repeat-flowering varieties of Climber. Strangely, if a variety is listed as being prone to mildew (such as Zéphirine Drouhin) it may be more successful grown in a slightly shaded position, because hot walls encourage mildew. Bare north-facing aspects exposed to the worst of the elements are not conducive to growing even the hardiest of roses, however, and you should not attempt this. The ultimate test for such conditions would be Maigold, a prickly spreader, more a Shrub than a Climber, and if this variety cannot be grown, then nothing else can.

▲ Altissimo is a Climber for all lovers of single roses. Here the colour of its blooms picks up that of the window. This variety can also be grown as a freestanding shrub by shortening the main stems at pruning time.

Climbing roses on pergolas, arches and pillars

▲ *Warm Welcome is one of the best patio climbers,*
the orange vermilion of its blooms beautifully set off
by bronze-red foliage. Here it is trained to clothe and
partially obscure this sculptural stone pyramid, a
focal point of the garden.

The traditional planting of roses on pergolas and arches calls for vigorous growers with a pliant habit which can be trained up the piers and across the top of the horizontal beams. The style of growth is the best criteria when choosing a variety for this purpose; obviously a rigid upright grower would not be suitable. Fragrance is also a desirable asset in roses grown over arches and pergolas under which people may walk and enjoy the sweet scent.

Ramblers were once used to clothe pergolas and arches, but they of course had a short mid-season flowering. The more recently introduced repeat-flowering Climbers are more appropriate and, given careful training (see page 161), the larger, more vigorous varieties are suitable even in small gardens. Since they do not have the pliant growth of the Ramblers, they will require gentle manipulation of their more rigid growths before age hardens the wood. Twining the upright growths round the piers will to a certain extent encourage bloom, but generally the same principles apply as in training Climbers horizontally to grow in a fan shape. On a pergola, there is no reason why summer-flowering Ramblers such as Dorothy Perkins may not be used in conjunction with a less vigorous repeat-flowering rose, ensuring a colourful 'roof' for the early part of the summer at least, while the vertical piers, clad in repeat-flowering varieties, can be colourful for longer. On a trellis pergola it makes sense to attach the shoots to the outside of the trellis rather than letting them weave through the latticework, so that the rose can easily be taken down whenever necessary for the purposes of pruning, maintenance and retraining.

Many rose catalogues refer to 'pillar' roses – these are particular selections with a neat, upright-growing habit which are less likely to shoot upwards, leaving a bare stem at the base of the plant. They are suitable for growing in restricted places which do not permit lateral growth, as well as for twining round to cover a freestanding pillar or obelisk. Growing Climbing roses on pillars, cones or obelisks is

▲ *Climbing rose Handel is trained up the metal framework of this gazebo, enclosing a magnificent terracotta vase filled with sempervivums.*

another useful way of adding height to a rose bed or border. In some gardens, a line of posts may be connected by draping heavy rope between their tops to form a continuous chain, along which Ramblers, with their lax growth, may be grown, turning the swathes of roses into an attractive feature when in flower.

Roses with large blooms may look out of proportion on small structures and smaller-flowered varieties will sometimes be a more suitable choice. The recently introduced Climbing Miniature roses, otherwise known as patio climbers, such as Laura Ford, Warm Welcome and Nice Day, would provide the right scale for the small garden,

though some of these are too short for tall pillars and pyramids. Varieties of patio climber are also useful on walls of restricted width, such as the space often found between windows or beside a front door, and may be excellent subjects to grow in containers where a paved area does not allow for planting directly into the soil. The containers should be at least 45cm/18in in height and diameter and provision must be made for supporting and training the roses' growth. You could either site the container against a wall to which you have fixed wires, or place a 'climbing frame' in the container itself.

In general, the old-fashioned Ramblers such as Albertine and Dorothy Perkins are difficult to fit into the smaller garden, having only a short flowering season in the early summer, being prone to mildew when it is rife and being difficult to prune properly to get the best results. Many of the more vigorous Climbing varieties are in fact quite large and therefore do not make good subjects for confined spaces. However, they do have their uses and their pliable stems can be trained into mature trees of 7m/23ft and more. Their vigorous stems will require some support to reach up into the branches as the rose should be planted at least 60cm/2ft away from the base of the tree trunk. Varieties suitable for this purpose and not mentioned elsewhere in this book are: *Rosa filipes* 'Kiftsgate' (a monster which will grow to some 10m/33ft and more), Rambling Rector, Alchymist, Wedding Day, Bobbie James and François Juranville. Of these, Alchymist is rather shrubby in habit but the flowers are a charming yellow-shaded gold, while François Juranville has flowers of salmon-pink; the other varieties are all white-flowered and they are possibly the more spectacular.

In recent years Karl Hetzel from Germany has bred a number of repeat-flowering Ramblers under the series names of Super Fairy, Super Dorothy, Super Elfin, Super Excelsa and Super Sparkle, which promise to be a great asset in the smaller garden. They are already becoming very popular in Europe, where they are sometimes budded on to stems to produce repeat-flowering weeping standards, and are likely to be available worldwide before long.

◄ *Hybrid Musk roses Buff Beauty and Felicia are both of a restrained height, making them suitable for a boundary hedge in this small country garden.*

Rose hedges

Rose hedges make an excellent structural feature in gardens large or small, providing colourful blooms for most of the summer. In rural surroundings, especially, there is immense scope for the use of a wide range of rose types, not necessarily of uniform height. Urban gardens may well call for a neater, more formal look, best achieved by selecting a compact-growing variety.

A hedge is only a line of plants doing a particular job: it could be merely 30cm/12in high, but might equally well be tree height. In a small garden we are of course considering the lower end of the scale, but much depends on the intended purpose. As knee-high hedges used to demarcate one part of the garden from another, without forming any part of a screen, the patio roses would be an excellent choice. One variety which would fit the bill superbly is Little Bo-Peep, whose blooms smother the whole plant − one of the main criteria of a rose hedge. Many bedding roses bloom only on top of the bush, which would not be at all suitable. Choose varieties which flower from the ground upwards, avoiding bare stems at the base.

To achieve the most homogeneous effect, stick to a single variety, but as long as the outline of the planting as a whole is regular, there is no reason why you cannot mix varieties, especially if you wish to create an informal appearance. In order, however, to avoid the look of planting a job-lot, it is a good idea to form a repeated pattern: ABABABAB, for example, or AABBAABBAABB, ABCABCABC or even ABCBABCBAB. Using a mix of varieties gives ample scope for you to be creative and as long as the pattern of the mix is consistent, it will have a sense of continuity. Many Shrub or English roses make excellent taller hedges. I once saw a spectacular, but unlikely, hedge comprising a Rugosa hybrid alternating with *Rosa moyesii* 'Geranium', the difference between the thicket of the Rugosa and the twiggy, upright growth of the briar contrasting well, especially when both were loaded with brilliant orange hips in late autumn.

▲ *The yellow-flowered English rose Graham Thomas, underplanted by geraniums and Alchemilla mollis, makes a good divider in an informal small garden.*

Many people plant a prickly rose hedge as an intruder-proof barrier which makes them feel secure and has the added bonus of blooms. Of reasonable proportions for a small garden, Rugosa hybrids such as Frau Dagmar Hastrup are very prickly, as are many of the Species roses. Rugosas, deeply planted, are good at regenerating shoots from the base which help to thicken the hedge at the bottom, enhancing its impenetrability Their brightly coloured hips and the golden tone of their autumn leaves are additional attractive features. Within the garden you may wish to screen off unsightly but necessary facilities, such as compost heaps, bonfire sites or sheds. Some of the taller Floribunda varieties, such as Iceberg or Mountbatten, make a good rose hedge for such a purpose.

Growing roses in containers

In the small garden roses may be grown in pots of all shapes and sizes to furnish a paved or gravelled area or to create effective 'punctuation' in the open garden. Indeed, the use of tubs and urns on a patio, terrace, balcony, wooden deck or rooftop is often the only way to grow roses in an urban area and containers such as these have the added advantage of being mobile. Give some thought to their placement: containers may be positioned to suit a formal style, used either singly as a focal point or arranged in pairs – for example, two pot-grown standard roses might flank a doorway or steps – otherwise they can be grouped or massed together in a more informal way.

Any rose will grow in a container, provided the volume of soil or potting compost is enough to sustain the size of plant. A patio rose, for instance, bought from the garden centre in a container of 4 litres, or measuring 12cm/5in across the top, needs to be replanted in at least double that volume of compost to carry it through a productive life. An average Climber or standard rose should be grown in a tub or pot with an inside diameter and depth of 50cm/20in. The foliage of Hybrid Teas and Floribundas is generally too tall, and their habit of growth too heavy, for pots in a small garden.

The choice of containers and the material from which they are made, whether they be terracotta or ceramic, stone

or wood, is a matter of personal preference. But the pot must have drainage holes drilled in the bottom and its base should be well-crocked. If it is standing on a flat surface, raise the pot off the ground just enough to allow any excess water to drain away. Choose a growing medium suitable for woody plants, preferably a compost based on the finest loam, adding well-rotted organic matter such as manure or garden compost and a source of potash (like ashes from a recent bonfire). Plant roses into their pots between autumn and early spring.

All the rules of good cultivation apply to roses grown in pots, since these plants depend totally on the attention you give them. Regular watering is essential, especially during dry weather; when you go on holiday, arrange for somebody else to water your containers. Roses need feeding during the growing season, so add a dash of liquid tomato food to the water at two-weekly intervals; its potash content will help ensure profuse blooming. Container-grown roses need light and air on all sides in order to develop evenly, so stand them slightly apart from other planting. Dead-head the blooms regularly and prune in late winter/early spring (see page 152).

Container-grown roses will eventually become pot-bound, their compost shrunk and compacted by continual watering. Once every two or three years, take them out of their containers in spring, knock off any old compost clinging to the roots and re-pot into fresh compost. In the intervening years pot-grown roses may be top-dressed, which involves removing a generous layer of old compost from the top of the container and replacing it with nutrient-rich new compost.

Choosing roses for containers

Used either on their own or in conjunction with other plants, container-grown roses will bring colour and life to a small garden in summer. Grown alone, many of the newer types of rose are ideally suited to container culture, especially patio roses, patio climbers and Ground Cover roses, with their small, neat foliage and fairly lax growth. The spreading habit of the more prostrate-growing varieties has also been used to great effect in hanging baskets. Plant in late autumn and leave the planted baskets outside until the roses become established. After this, if you have an unheated glasshouse,

▲ *An informal collection of potted plants in galvanized containers, including standard and patio roses, brings colour and interest to this corner of a contemporary paved garden.*

◄ *Their colours, shapes and fragrance make roses an ideal subject to grow in containers on a rooftop garden. The popular Floribunda, Iceberg, plays an important role in introducing long-lasting fragrance and colour.*

◀ Container-grown Ground Cover roses are deliberately placed to echo the formality of the clipped hedge, bringing a touch of colour to the garden without detracting from the strict geometric layout.

▶ The County Series of Ground Cover roses are successfully grown in hanging baskets. Hertfordshire, with carmine-red blooms, and Gwent, pale yellow, make an eye-catching display. Three or four plants, preferably of one variety, are ideal for a basket of 32–35cm/ 12–14in diameter. The roots of bare-rooted plants may need trimming to make them sit well.

they can be brought in and the early growths may be 'assisted' to trail downwards over the edge of the basket. (If you do not have a greenhouse, leave them outside but bear in mind that they will not bloom until mid- to late summer.) Once all danger of frost is over, move the baskets outside. Water daily, adding a weekly feed of tomato food, with a high potash content, to feed both foliage and flowers.

In larger containers the planting need not be restricted to roses used singly but companions need to be selected with care. In a group planting, choose from the multitude of rose shapes, sizes and colours to contrast, or blend with, the enormous selection of well-textured foliage plants. Bear scale in mind at all times. It would be pointless to use the dainty, small-flowered varieties of patio or China roses in conjunction with a large, glossy-leaved fatshedera, for example. Choice of colour is always crucial to the impact of a display too. If the background is dark in tone, you may wish to select a pale-coloured rose to lift and brighten the area and so that the blooms show up well against it.

Ideas for the best roses to grow successfully in both containers and hanging baskets are suggested (right).

Variety	Code	Use	Colour
Avon	POULmulti	PB	White
Crystal Palace*	POULrek	P	Creamy peach
Festival*	KORdialo	P	Crimson and white
Gwent*	POULurt	PB	Lemon-yellow
Hertfordshire	KORtenay	PB	Carmine-pink
Kent*	POULcov	P	White
Lancashire*	KORstesgli	PB	Crimson
Little Bo-peep	POULlen	P	Palest pink
Little White Pet		P	White
Mandarin*	KORcelin	P	Orange and pink
Pink Hit	POULtipe	P	Soft rose-pink
Queen Mother*	KORquemu	P	Soft pink
Saint Boniface	KORmatt	P	Brilliant scarlet
Suffolk	KORmixal	PB	Crimson
The Fairy*		P	Soft pink
Top Marks	FRYministar	P	Vermilion-scarlet
Wiltshire*	KORmuse	PB	Bright rose-pink
White Flower Carpet*	NOASchnee	PB	White
Worcestershire	KORalon	PB	Pale lemon

* = featured in this book   P = roses for pots   B = roses for baskets

Companions for roses

▲ *The delicate flowers of* Clematis '*Hybrida Sieboldii*' *enhance the soft pink blooms of Climbing rose New Dawn, one of the first repeat-flowering Climbers. Take care choosing varieties of clematis, which may need a pruning regime detrimental to that of roses. Different forms of Jackmanii and Viticella clematis, which can be pruned almost to the ground in late winter or early spring, are the best to use.*

The multitude of colours and forms within the rose genus can be embellished in the garden by the introduction of contrasting or complementary plants from other families. Apart from contributing to a rich and varied border planting, companion plants are valuable for a number of reasons. They may be chosen to flower at a different season, to provide interest when the roses are not in bloom, or simultaneous-flowering subjects may be selected specifically to enhance and offset the summer display of roses. Tall-growing shrubs will bring structure to a border, while low-growing subjects like spring bulbs and early summer perennials will shroud the bare stems of some roses, providing interest at ground level.

There are, it is true, some drawbacks to the practice of underplanting roses. Mulching is made more difficult by threatening to smother low-growing plants, and there will be problems in applying much-needed food to your roses if the underplanting is too thick. Repeat-flowering roses do not generally cope too well with very close competition from other plants, so it is important to allow your roses ample space, without spoiling the line and flow of a mixed border. However, all these disadvantages pale into insignificance against the beauty of a well-planted mixed border.

The bold and sculptural shape of many roses, their relatively large flower size, long flowering season and wide range of colours gives them a vital role in the successful mixed border, where at least a third of the shrubs will be roses. In choosing companion plants for roses, bear in mind their height and flower shape as well as colour, flowering time, foliage, texture and perfume. While plants used at the front of a border need only be tall enough to hide any of the rose's bare stems, those at the back or centre of the bed should have some structural value. The blooms of companion plants are usually smaller than those of the surrounding roses and may take an entirely different, contrasting form, such as the spikes of delphiniums and foxgloves or the feathery forms of gypsophila and *Crambe cordifolia*. Partnering roses with plants that have similar

flower forms, like peonies and cistus, can, if there is a subtle colour contrast and a difference in height, provide a shapely echo, although using large-flowered peonies with roses in a bed, or clematis hybrids with dinner-plate sized blooms to partner Climbing roses on a wall, may not have the desired impact. In terms of underplanting, avoid invasive ground-covering plants such as ivies, bluebells and Solomon's seal which would deprive the roses of moisture and nutrients.

In early spring bulbs bring colour to a bed before roses even break into young growth. There is a range of crocuses, from white, through cream and shades of yellow to mauves and deep purples, as well as delicate white snowdrops and blue muscari. The later spring bulbs – daffodils, narcissi and tulips – can look wonderful peering through Ground Cover roses, and, by the time they are over, the roses will have started into growth, their leaves hiding the shrivelling,

▲ Roses play a key part in this mixed border, with its variety of textures, colours and shapes. The blooms of Little White Pet contrast effectively with the tall spires of foxgloves and the domes of clipped box, while pillar roses give height at the back of the bed.

▶ *In this vibrant colour scheme, the yellow spires of verbascum and the lime-yellow leaves of golden hop offset the grey upright foliage of lychnis and the green leaves of the roses. The bright pink lychnis flowers and the rounded blooms of the scarlet Floribunda make a startling contrast.*

unsightly bulb foliage and allowing rejuvenating bulbs to mature naturally. Spring-flowering shrubs are useful partners too, providing interest even before, or at the same time as, the earliest Species roses. Early-flowering spiraeas, forsythia and flowering currants (*Ribes*) may be somewhat hackneyed but provide effective splashes of colour, followed by the gloriously fragrant lilacs in white, cream, pink and purple.

Herbaceous perennials are classic summer-flowering subjects to plant amid Shrub roses in the mixed border. The tall spires of foxgloves, delphiniums and hollyhocks give vertical relief to the rounded clumps of rose bushes. Among summer-flowering bulbs a range of lilies give an exotic touch, introducing a different range of hues. Late summer brings yet another flush of colour to the garden in the form of asters, phlox, valerian, *Sedum spectabile* and *Anemone japonica*, followed by the crop of yellows, golds, oranges and scarlets of autumn foliage and rose hips, haws and brilliant berries.

When choosing partners, much depends on the type and habit of the roses in your mixed border. The vivid colours and hard lines of some Modern bedding roses, such as Hybrid Teas and Floribundas, can make them unsympathetic companions when used singly. They are better planted in small groups, choosing colours that complement their surroundings, with some mounded, bushy plants nearby to help disguise their rigid habit. Group planting in clumps avoids the confetti-like look of single planting and makes a greater impact. It also prevents single roses getting lost in the abundant growth of other plants. Shrub roses, on the other hand, are often planted singly. A Shrub rose with rounded growth can become the focus in a border, while those with tall, arching growth, such as *Rosa moyesii* and *Rosa glauca*, or even Hybrid Tea roses Alexander and Congratulations, form an excellent contrast to lower plants. Old Shrub and English roses are best partnered by herbaceous perennials that contrast with or complement their rounded form and full, multi-petalled blooms. Roses look wonderful emerging from lower-growing plants like aquilegias or the light, feathery flowers of gypsophila or *Alchemilla mollis*, all of which set off the heavier, more 'blobby' growth and flowers of Shrub roses.

Colour combinations

One of the rose's great virtues is the wide range of colour found within the genus and its many species and hybrids. In selecting companions, your aim is to find simultaneously flowering perennials, shrubs and bulbs which pick up the colour of the rose and enhance it, or to choose contrasting-colour plants to act as a foil for roses. In mixed borders, a more subtle effect is produced if colour changes are achieved gradually, in drifts, rather than jumping abruptly from one colour to another.

Foliage colour should also be taken into account in a mixed planting as it can become an important backdrop for roses. The silver leaves of *Stachys byzantina*, artemisias and santolinas as well as the glaucous leaves of lavender, senecio and *Ruta graveolens* all provide an ideal foil for roses of all shades, while the golden-yellow shades found in many evergreen euonymus would completely kill the delicacy of a soft pink rose such as The Fairy or Cécile Brünner. On the other hand, either the golden-yellow or the silvery grey of lavender and artemisia would form a tasteful combination with a cream or yellow rose such as Gwent or Crystal Palace.

When thinking of colour for contrast, one immediately turns to the various shades of blue, one of the hues missing from the spectrum of colours found among garden roses. The blue flower spikes of lavender in its many varieties blend beautifully with all shades of pink-flowered rose. Among the hardy perennials, the colours of *Geranium* 'Johnson's Blue' and *G.* 'Buxton's Blue', of the hardy agapanthus, the various campanulas and catmint (*Nepeta* x *faassenii*) complement all shades of pink rose except, perhaps, salmon-pink. Pure yellows also provide a good contrast to rich blues, the paler shades verging on cream associating better with soft blues. Purple foliage is also a good partner for pink roses: as found, for example, in low-growing *Ajuga reptans* 'Atropurpurea' and dark violas as well as the taller *Cotinus coggygria* and *Cosmos atrosanguineus*.

Whether we want to complement, blend with or even tone down the impact of the brilliant vermilions and orange-reds of rose blooms, there are many plants to choose among the perennials, such as coreopsis, rudbeckia, daylilies and some of the shorter-growing sunflowers as well as heliopsis, another yellow daisy. Among the bedding annuals try such subjects as the marigolds – French marigolds, pot marigolds and African marigolds, as well as

Tagetes (often grown among roses to attract hoverflies which are deadly enemies to that garden pest, the aphid). The deep reds and stronger pinks generally look best next to purples and mauves. The yellow found in Modern roses can sometimes be difficult to accommodate; if it is harsh and garish, it will jar with most other flowers. But try yellow roses with bronze fennel and other plants with bronze-tinged foliage, as well as with blue-flowered plants such as *Salvia* x *superbum*, delphiniums or blue penstemons.

▲ *White lightens up a planting and adds a touch of elegance to a mixed border.* Geranium *'Kashmir White' here shrouds the base of a full-petalled rose.*

▲ *The texture of flowing grasses emphasizes the glowing crimson blooms of patio rose Festival.*

a collection of roses

Over the following pages will be found close-up photographic portraits of the best roses for small gardens, showing their unique qualities and characteristics. They are divided into Hybrid Teas, Floribundas, Climbing Roses, Ground Cover Roses, Shrub Roses and English Roses and individual descriptions can be found grouped together at the end of each section. Under the name of the rose variety are other names it may be known by including, first, its international code name, which comprises the name of the breeder in its first three or four letters; where no code name is given, this rose predates the practice of giving international names. Following each description is a summary of the rose's vital statistics: its size (spread followed by height); the name of the breeder and the year it first appeared; named parents where known; any major awards received; and whether it has any fragrance. The abbreviations used for the awards are explained in detail on page 24.

hybrid teas

ROYAL WILLIAM

Still the best dark red rose, with
perfectly reflexed outer petals.

SELFRIDGES

A worldwide favourite for its fragrance and glorious colour.

CLEOPATRA

An upright grower with dark foliage, which lasts well as a cut flower.

INGRID BERGMAN
Classic blooms are borne in
great profusion.

JUST JOEY

A strong, bushy grower with large, frilly-edged blooms.

CONGRATULATIONS

An excellent rose for cutting, with
long, smooth stems.

VALENCIA

Large, sweetly scented buff-orange blooms, twice the size shown here.

PEACE

Surely one of the greatest roses of all time (shown here less than half its actual size).

DAWN CHORUS

Neat, fragrant blooms of a classic high-pointed shape (here enlarged to three times its size).

SILVER JUBILEE

One of the best roses of the twentieth century,
with beautiful scrolled blooms.

TEQUILA SUNRISE

A spectacular cocktail of a rose, appropriately named.

TYNWALD

An upright-growing rose whose rounded
buds open to large, many-petalled blooms.

hybrid teas

Previously known as Large-Flowered roses, this class of rose has now reverted to its original name, Hybrid Tea. The first popular varieties were introduced in the latter part of the nineteenth century, the early cultivars a result of crossing Hybrid Perpetuals with Tea roses, hence the name used in the early classification. It is extremely unlikely, however, that any modern Large-Flowered rose has a Tea rose in its parentage or even its ancestry. The stiff, upright-growing Hybrid Teas, with their scrolled buds and pointed blooms, differed greatly from the rosette-shaped roses of the past and were the start of a completely new approach to growing roses.

These bedding varieties of rose have classic-shaped flowers borne mainly at the top of the plant, either singly or in well-spaced clusters of two or three blooms. The blooms can vary from the slim, neat, high-centred shape offered by florists as a cut flower, to large, full, multi-petalled blooms. The plants themselves may be either upright, elegant specimens growing up to 60cm/2ft tall, or bushy, many-branched shrubby growers or, finally, tall, stately bushes up to 2m/6ft in height.

The early colours of red, pink and white were enhanced by the addition of yellow and orange in the early 1900s, and the luminous cinnabar-reds in the 1950s, which in turn gave rise to the brilliant vermilion-scarlets of today. By careful yet rigorous selection, varieties have been chosen to produce blooms in quantity possessing characteristics that make ideal cut flowers with their elegant, high-pointed scrolled shape. The qualities looked for in a 'florist's' cut flower show colour from the moment the bud opens and the petals remain crisp and unfading for a long time, even when the flowers themselves crumple and die.

CLEOPATRA *Page 55*

Synonyms KORverpea; Kleopatra, New Kleopatra, Peace of Vereennigen

Not to be confused with an earlier (1950s) variety of the same name, the same colour and – to make matters even more confusing – from the same raiser. This Cleopatra is an upright grower with fine, high-centred blooms of medium size, sometimes borne in clusters though more often not. The blooms are glowing crimson-scarlet within and deep harvest gold on the reverse of the petals. The deep bronze-green foliage is tinted reddish bronze when young and, together with the dark purplish stems, makes a perfect foil for the blooms. A good variety for cutting.

Size *50cm/20in × 75cm/2ft 6in*
Raiser *Kordes Germany 1994*
Award *TGC, RNRS*
Slight fragrance

CONGRATULATIONS *Page 58*

Synonyms KORlift; Sylvia

A tall-growing rose, sometimes classified as a Floribunda, though it tends to grow its flowers singly on a stem rather than in clusters. Its height makes it eminently suited to planting towards the back of a border. The clear rose-pink blooms of elegant classic shape are borne on long, smooth, almost thornless stems. They last for almost a week when cut, making Congratulations a deserved favourite among flower arrangers.

A paler pink sport (mutation) of this variety was chosen by the National Association of Flower Arrangers Societies (NAFAS) to celebrate its thirtieth anniversary, under the appropriate name, Pink Pearl. The matt foliage is pale green, shaded maroon when young.

Size *60cm/2ft × 120cm/4ft*
Raiser *Kordes Germany 1979*
Parentage *Carina × seedling*
Slight fragrance

DAWN CHORUS *Page 60*

Synonym DICquasar

The neat, crisply petalled scented blooms of Dawn Chorus are borne in quite large, well-spaced clusters on a medium height bush of compact bushy habit. The classic high-pointed flowers are extremely long lasting and have become popular among flower arrangers who do not mind the relatively short stems.

The coppery-red foliage makes an admirable foil for the tangerine and bright orange-yellow blooms of exquisite shape. A popular bedding rose selected by the British rose growing industry as their Rose of the Year in 1993.

Size *60cm/2ft × 60cm/2ft*
Raiser *Dickson U.K. 1993*
Parentage *Wishing × Peer Gynt*
Awards *Gold Medal Dublin 1993; Certificate of Merit Glasgow 1995*
Fragrant

INGRID BERGMAN *Page 56*

Synonym POULman

The large, glowing dark red blooms of Ingrid Bergman represent a fine tribute to one of the classic beauties of the film industry. The scroll-shaped flowers are borne erect on sturdy stems, making this rose excellent for cutting and for exhibiting. But its real virtue lies in the extreme weather resistance of the crisp petals, turning it into an asset for any rose bed or mixed border. It is well furnished with glossy, dark green foliage. The blooms also have a slight scent, though not the deep, luscious fragrance one expects from a red rose.

Size *60cm/2ft × 90cm/3ft*
Raiser *Poulsen Denmark 1986*
Awards *TGC, RNRS; Gold Medal Belfast*
Slight fragrance

JUST JOEY *Page 57*

Coppery orange-red, high-pointed buds open to exciting frilly-edged, extra large apricot-buff blooms which, as they open, develop pink shading at the edge of the petals. The open, rather loosely angular plant is well clothed in matt bronze-red leaves maturing to deepest bronze-green.

This well known and highly popular variety was named by its raiser after his wife. It was voted 'World's Favourite Rose' by a congress of the World Federation of Rose Societies in New Zealand in 1994.

Size *60cm/2ft x 60cm/2ft*

Raiser *R. Pawsey (Cants of Colchester)*
U.K. 1973
Awards *TGC, RNRS; JMMM 1994*
Fragrant

PEACE *Page 59*

Synonyms Gloria Dei, Madame A.
Meilland, Gioia

One of the most famous roses of all
time and possibly the best loved,
although there are no doubt some who
would disagree.

Peace is a large grower whose strong
constitution makes it a taller plant than
many gardeners anticipate, especially when
it is not pruned. Raised in the late 1930s,
Peace was not introduced until after the
end of the Second World War, when it
was presented at the inaugural assembly of
the United Nations, hence the name.

The slightly fragrant blooms can be
among the largest in the rose garden,
somewhat changeable in colour with
different soil conditions and climates.
It has in fact produced several mutations
of colour during its long life.

The large, rounded buds are usually
deep yellow with splashes of red opening
to large, frilly, pale yellow blooms lightly
edged pink. The heavy leathery foliage is
deep glossy green.
Size *120cm/4ft x 120cm/4ft*
Raiser *Meilland France 1939*
Awards *Gold Medal RNRS; Award of*
Garden Merit, RHS; many others
Light fragrance

ROYAL WILLIAM *Page 53*

Synonyms KORzaun; Duftzauber '84',
Fragrant Charm, Leonore Christian

The deep crimson blooms have the
classical shape with perfectly reflexed
outer petals. The fragrance is the
luscious fruity perfume one expects
from the crimson roses, yet the petals are
crisp and unfading. What makes this
such an outstanding rose is the robust
and healthy growth with disease-resistant
foliage, deep maroon-red when young,
ageing to dark bronze-green.

Selected by the British rose growing
industry as their Rose of the Year in
1987, it was also awarded the James
Mason Memorial Medal for having given
special pleasure to rose-loving gardeners
in 1999.
Size *60cm/2ft x 90cm/3ft*
Raiser *Kordes Germany 1984*
Parentage *Feuerzauber x seedling*
Awards *Award of Garden Merit, RHS; TGC,*
RNRS; JMMM 1999
Very fragrant

SELFRIDGES *Page 54*

Synonyms KORpriwa; Berolina

Bright yellow with amber-yellow shading,
the blooms are of good shape and size.
The sweet 'Tea' fragrance has made this a
yellow rose to cherish, though its
extreme vigour will often produce canes
of almost 2m/6ft in height, so it will
require careful placing at the back of the
border. The semi-glossy foliage is bright

green and it is a fine rose for cutting
because of the long, smooth stems and
very few thorns.

The name 'Selfridges' came from the
London Oxford Street store of that
name to celebrate the centenary of the
birth of Gordon Selfridge, its founder.
Size *60cm/2ft x 120cm/4ft and more*
Raiser *Kordes Germany 1984*
Awards *ADR 1986*
Fragrant

SILVER JUBILEE *Page 61*

A superb variety with spectacular
blooms borne in great profusion.
Although it is primarily a rose most
suited for bedding, providing a mass of
colour, the blooms when disbudded
become quite large and will win prizes
on the show bench.

The colour may be described as
apricot-salmon shades with a deeper
reverse, while rose-pink is often to be
seen within the petals. The distinctive
mid-green foliage is large and luxuriant.
The plant, upright yet bushy, is a
handsome specimen though well-
endowed with thorns.

Named to commemorate the Silver
Jubilee of H.M. Queen Elizabeth II, this
rose is also a fitting memorial to its
raiser the late Alec Cocker of Aberdeen.
Size *60cm/2ft x 75cm/2ft 6in*
Raiser *Cocker U.K. 1978*
Parentage *[(Highlight x Colour Wonder) x*
(Parkdirektor Riggers x Piccadilly)] x Mischief

Awards *PIT, RNRS 1977; Gold Medal Portland, Oregon 1981; JMMM 1985*
Some fragrance

TEQUILA SUNRISE *Page 62*

Synonyms DICobey; Beaulieu

A spectacular cocktail of a rose, its petals, dark and bunched-up when in tight bud, explode to reveal a deep golden-yellow bloom heavily edged and shaded brilliant scarlet, developing into a tangerine-orange shade as the bloom matures. The glossy bronze-green foliage is lightly tinted maroon in its juvenile stage and smothers the compact-growing plant. The blooms are sometimes borne in shapely clusters and other times singly. A fascinating variety to cut and watch closely as it opens.

Size *60cm/2ft x 60cm/2ft*
Raiser *Dickson N. Ireland 1989*
Awards *Gold Medal, RNRS 1988; Gold Medal Belfast*
Slight fragrance

TYNWALD *Page 63*

Synonym MATtwyt

A tall, upright rose with distinctive rounded buds of ivory-white, lightly tinted pale lemon-yellow, often borne in clusters but mostly singly. They open to large, rounded, many-petalled blooms initially giving the impression of a white rose but on closer examination proving to be delicately shaded lemon-yellow and soft pink in the inner folds of the petals.

Often growing quite tall, this rose is suited to a position at the back of a border and, if pruned with care, it can grow into a tall handsome shrub.

It was named in 1979 to commemorate the millennium of Tynwald, the Manx (Isle of Man, U.K.) parliament, the oldest continuous legislature in the world.

Size *60cm/2ft x 120cm/4ft*
Raiser *Mattock U.K. 1979*
Parentage *Peer Gynt x Isis*
Fragrant

VALENCIA *Page 59*

Synonyms KOReklia; New Valencia, Valeccia

Very large blooms of buff-orange with golden shading are often of such exquisite form that Valencia receives top prizes in flower shows. The fine sweet and fruity fragrance endures, inviting people to bury their nose in the multitude of petals. A good rose for cutting, Valencia flowers continuously throughout the summer and into autumn, though it can suffer damage in wet weather, when its blooms may 'ball up'. A vigorous grower, it could be placed in the middle of a rose bed or border.

Size *60cm/2ft x 90cm/3ft*
Raiser *Kordes Germany 1989*
Awards *HE Medal for fragrance 1989; Gold Medal RNRS*
Very fragrant

floribundas

SHOCKING BLUE

An incredible fragrance in an unusual colour.

FELLOWSHIP

The fragrant, hot-coloured
blooms are a real eye-catcher.

SUNSET BOULEVARD

Especially good seen against a dark
evergreen background.

INTRIGUE

One of the darkest red roses, its semi-double blooms are borne in large clusters.

TRUMPETER

A low bushy grower whose blooms are
as jazzy as its namesake (shown here
twice its actual size).

ANNA LIVIA

A fine bedding rose that
is deservedly popular for
its even growth and
showy blooms (in reality
two-thirds of the size
shown here).

FASCINATION

Named Rose of the Year in 1999, this beautiful compact-growing variety is ideal for a small garden. It is shown here at half its true size.

THE TIMES

A fine bedding rose with a well-deserved reputation for good health.

SWEET DREAM

An attractive soft-coloured
variety for a limited space.

ORANGES AND LEMONS

A scented rose with an exotic difference.

QUEEN MOTHER

An elegant rose named to celebrate
Her Majesty's ninetieth birthday.

FESTIVAL

A neat, rounded grower
with luxuriant foliage.

CRYSTAL PALACE

A low-growing cluster-flowered
rose with larger blooms than
most patio roses (actually twice
the size shown).

KORRESIA

One of the sweetest perfumed
roses, unusual in a yellow variety.

MANDARIN

A whorl of petals showing a remarkable blend of
colours (shown here four times its real size).

ICEBERG

Still one of the best white
roses ever produced.

HANNAH GORDON

Perfectly formed blooms in well-shaped clusters,
here shown at four times its actual size.

floribundas

Formerly named Cluster-flowered roses, Floribunda bedding roses bear their flowers in trusses or clusters with many blooms opening at the same time. The great trusses of bloom that are characteristic of the Floribundas are influenced by the Polyantha Pom-poms (now rarely grown because of their susceptibility to mildew), with a petal texture inherited from their Hybrid Tea forebears. Even further back in their ancestry the China rose had a strong influence. Floribunda flowers provide massed drifts of colour through the garden, rather than producing individual specimens of perfect shape for close scrutiny. In truth, however, the inflorescences of many Floribunda varieties are quite as beautiful as their larger-flowered relatives.

The size and shape of bloom can vary enormously, from the dainty five-petalled varieties reminiscent of their wild rose ancestors, to the shapely, many-petalled specimens so close to the large-flowered Hybrid Tea roses. The height does not form any part of the definition of a Floribunda. These plants may range from the dwarf cultivars, now classified separately as patio roses, to giants which may reach 2m/6ft high, or even taller if left unpruned, such as 'The Queen Elizabeth' rose. Some Floribundas, though not many, have inherited a fragrance that is quite as good as anything else to be found in the rose world.

The patio roses, selected from dwarf (up to 50cm/20in) compact-growing Floribundas and larger-growing Miniature roses, are popular in modern gardens. They are ideal to grow in containers to enhance paved areas where direct planting would be impossible, or where the only room available is in small beds in which the larger Hybrid Teas and Floribundas would be out of place. Patio roses are also excellent subjects for planting at the front of shrub borders as well as for edging paths. Many fine patio varieties are also sold as pot plants which, given care and attention, will add colour to conservatory plantings and for short periods of time may be grown as house plants.

ANNA LIVIA *Page 74*

Synonyms KORmetter; Sandton Beauty, Trier 2000

The large double rose-pink blooms have the merest hint of salmon, although it takes a keen eye to detect it. The clusters of bloom are particularly well shaped, often with ten or more flowers in the truss at one time.

This showy variety is quite awe-inspiring when planted en masse. The bushy plant produces very even growth, making Anna Livia one of the best bedding varieties. It has a light, refreshing fragrance.

The name 'Anna Livia' is taken from James Joyce's book *Finnegan's Wake* and commemorates the millennium of Dublin, the Irish capital, in 1998.

Size *60cm/2ft × 75cm/2ft 6in*
Raiser *Kordes Germany 1985*
Parentage *(seedling × Tornado) × seedling*
Awards *Award of Garden Merit, RHS; Gold Medal Glasgow 1991; Gold Medal Orléans 1987*
Light fragrance

CRYSTAL PALACE *Page 81*

Synonyms POULrek; Cristel Palace

Patio rose. A low-growing cluster-flowered variety somewhat different to the other patio roses in that the blooms are larger and the bush less compact. The delightful blooms have been described as 'light peachy cream' in colour and its delicate shading gives the variety its great and unique charm.

Size *60cm/2ft × 60cm/2ft*
Raiser *Poulsen Denmark 1995*
Slight fragrance

FASCINATION *Page 76*

Synonym POULmax

Dark green glossy foliage clothes this bedding rose which bears attractive clusters of fragrant coral-pink blooms. This neat, compact grower makes a superb subject for the smaller garden, whether grown in beds or borders of limited size, or in planters such as large urns or pots.

After two years of exhaustive testing by the British rose industry, this variety was chosen as their 'Rose of the Year' in 1999.

Size *60cm/2ft × 60cm/2ft*
Raiser *Poulsen Denmark 1999*
Fragrant

FELLOWSHIP *Page 70*

Synonyms HARwelcome; Livin' Easy

One of the brightest coloured Floribunda roses, the glowing orange-vermilion flowers are freely produced in shapely clusters. The well-formed Hybrid Tea-shaped buds open to cupped blooms with attractive rounded petals, revealing golden stamens.

This vigorous bushy plant, well clothed with dark shiny foliage, is reputedly very disease resistant. For those who admire 'hot' colours, it is an excellent choice to enliven a dull (but not shady) spot in the garden, though it is not for the faint hearted!

Size *60cm/2ft × 75cm/2ft 6in*
Raiser *Harkness U.K. 1992*
Parentage *Southampton × Remember Me*
Awards *Gold Medal RNRS; AARS 1996; Gold Medal Portland, Oregon 1998*
Slight fragrance

FESTIVAL *Page 81*

Synonym KORdialo

Patio rose. An attractive variety bearing large clusters of blooms 5–8cm/2–3in across. They are bright crimson-scarlet with a silvery white reverse to the petals, giving a bicoloured appearance to the opening buds. The crimson flower then opens with a silvery white zone at the heart, accenting the golden boss of stamens.

This low-growing, rounded bush makes an ideal subject for planting at the edge of a flower bed or in a planter. The foliage is dark holly-green with an attractive gloss.

Size *45cm /18in × 45cm/18in*
Raiser *Kordes Germany 1993*
Parentage *Regensberg × seedling*
Awards *TGC, RNRS; Rose of the Year 1994*
Slight fragrance

HANNAH GORDON *Page 85*

Synonyms KORweiso; Raspberry Ice

A delightful confection of shades of pink varying from palest blush, almost

white, within the flower, to deep cherry-pink on the edges of the petals. The shades vary, depending on the intensity of sunlight, and deepen as the bloom ages. The flowers are borne in well-spaced moderately sized clusters on an upright-growing bush.

The shape of the flower buds, their exotic colouring and the sparsely thorned stems make this cluster-flowered rose popular for use as a cut flower. It is an excellent variety for all gardens.

Size *60cm/2ft x 75cm/2ft 6in*
Raiser *Kordes Germany 1983*
Parentage *seedling x Bordure (Strawberry Ice)*
Awards *TGC, RNRS 1983*
Slight fragrance

ICEBERG *Page 84*

Synonyms KORbin; Fée des Neige, Schneewittchen

Introduced in 1958, Iceberg is still one of the most widely planted roses. This bushy, almost shrubby grower has semi-double, well-formed pure white flowers. Sometimes the white flowers display a slight blush, especially in cooler weather, and, as with all white roses, any damage is immediately visible; for example, raindrops which do not dry off straight away may leave pink spots. The flowers, which are borne in clusters of up to a dozen at one time, have a delicate wild-rose perfume.

Iceberg can be used for many purposes: as a bedding rose, as a Shrub rose and as a hedge; as a standard (Tree) rose it is among the best. It has even produced a climbing sport which is most useful, spreading as it does to some 4–5m/12–15ft and flowering at the height of summer.

Size *75cm/2ft 6in x 110cm/3ft 6in*
Raiser *Kordes Germany 1958*
Parentage *Robin Hood x Virgo*
Awards *Gold Medal RNRS 1958; Gold Medal Baden Baden 1983; Award of Garden Merit, RHS; World's Favourite Rose 1983*
Slight fragrance

INTRIGUE *Page 72*

Synonyms KORlech; Lavaglut, Lavaglow

One of the deepest red roses currently offered in rose catalogues. It should not be confused with an American-raised variety of the same name, which is reddish purple. The large clusters of blackish crimson blooms often have up to 24 flowers. These semi-double blooms are particularly beautiful when seen in strong sunlight and retain their colour until they drop.

A strong, bushy grower of medium height well clothed in dark bronze-green foliage, it is an excellent rose for all gardens due to its almost non-stop performance during the flowering season, from midsummer until the first frosts of autumn.

Size *60cm/2ft x 60cm/2ft*
Raiser *Kordes Germany 1981*
Parentage *Gruss an Bayern x seedling*

Awards *TGC, RNRS 1980*
Slight fragrance

KORRESIA *Page 82*

Synonyms KORresia; Friesia, Sunsprite

Still one of the best yellow bedding roses. The large Hybrid Tea-shaped blooms are borne, sometimes singly and sometimes in clusters, in close succession and are of brilliant clear yellow which – rare for a rose in this colour – does not fade. Another unusual feature of Korresia is that it has a strong fragrance, which has won it awards.

A vigorous, bushy plant of average height, it is well furnished with an abundance of glossy, bright green foliage and makes an excellent hedge. The blooms shatter on maturity, making dead-heading unnecessary.

Size *60cm/2ft x 75cm/2ft 6in*
Raiser *Kordes Germany 1977*
Parentage *Friedrich Worlein x Spanish Sun*
Awards *James Alexander Gamble Award for fragrance 1979; JMMM 1989; Gold Medal Baden Baden*
Very fragrant

MANDARIN *Page 83*

Synonym KORcelin

Patio rose. Shades of gold, orange, pink and even red are shot through the small rosette-shaped flowers of this neat little bush. As the blooms open fully, the pink is accentuated as the orange grows paler and the rosette becomes denser when the

petals take on a slightly fluted appearance. The dark stems are stiffly upright and are furnished with attractive dark green foliage, making this a superb subject for a small rose bed set in a terrace or other paved area.

Size *45cm/18in* x *45cm/18in*
Raiser *Kordes Germany 1987*
Awards *Gold Medal Glasgow 1994; Certificate of Merit, Dublin*
Slight fragrance

ORANGES AND LEMONS
Page 79
Synonyms MACanlorem; Papagena

A rose for those looking for something exotic, perhaps for a hot-coloured bed. Large, full blooms of golden yellow with stripes and flecks of deep tangerine-orange are carried in small clusters on a taller than average bush. The long stems make this a suitable Floribunda for cutting, introducing something special for the flower arranger.

The deep bronze-green, glossy foliage is tinted reddish purple when young. The taller shoots, when trained, can turn Oranges and Lemons into a shrub or even a short pillar rose.

Size *60cm/2ft* x *110cm/3ft 6in*
Raiser *McGredy New Zealand 1993*
Parentage *Roller Coaster* x *New Year (Arcadian)*
Awards *TGC, RNRS 1991*
Slight fragrance

QUEEN MOTHER   *Page 80*
Synonyms KORquemu; Queen Mum

Patio rose. A delightfully elegant rose chosen to celebrate Her Majesty's ninetieth birthday, this variety naturally became a popular choice when the Queen Mother achieved her century in the year 2000.

The simple, semi-double soft pink blooms have great charm, showing up well against the glossy dark green foliage. This vigorous shrubby plant of low to medium height is a fine variety, showing a distinct relationship to a host of recently bred Kordes varieties with their characteristic resistance to disease.

Size *60cm/2ft* x *60cm/2ft*
Raiser *Kordes Germany 1991*
Awards *Award of Garden Merit, RHS; ADR 1991*
Delicate fragrance

SHOCKING BLUE   *Page 69*
Synonym KORblue

One of the best of the so-called 'blue' roses. Shocking Blue was first introduced in Germany as a cut flower variety but, having been tested in the garden, it soon found favour among gardeners looking for something out of the ordinary. The magenta buds are shaded and splashed deep plum-purple and the opening petals reveal a rich lilac-magenta flower with a very heavy scent.

To get the full benefit of the unusual shade it is a good idea to plant it

alongside a lemon-yellow flower or golden-foliaged plant, otherwise the colour does not stand out sufficiently against its deep bronze-green foliage. As with many varieties, it requires dead-heading to ensure continuity of bloom.

Size *60cm/2ft* x *110cm/3ft 6in*
Raiser *Kordes Germany 1985*
Parentage *Silver Star* x *seedling*
Very fragrant

SUNSET BOULEVARD
Page 71
Synonym HARbabble

Named to celebrate and publicize the musical play of the same name, 'Sunset Boulevard' was selected by the British rose industry as their Rose of the Year in 1997.

Well-shaped elegant buds of glowing orange-salmon open to reveal an intriguing shade of orange-apricot amid crisp unfolding petals. The slightly fragrant blooms are borne continuously on an upright but compact-growing plant, well-furnished with mid-green semi-matt foliage. This variety is seen at its best against a dark green background.

Size *60cm/2ft* x *75cm/2ft 6in*
Raiser *Harkness U.K. 1997*
Parentage *Harold MacMillan* x *Fellowship*
Awards *TGC, RNRS 1996; Rose of the Year 1997*
Slight fragrance

SWEET DREAM *Page 78*

Synonyms FRYminicot; Sweet Dreams

Patio rose. Clusters of creamy apricot round buds open to reveal rosette-shaped, peachy-apricot coloured blooms with deeper shades within the unfurling petals. The clusters may vary from just two or three to a whole wide-spreading head of many blooms borne on a strong upright stem. The plants often send up quite tall shoots and some have even been trained as mini-climbers, but if you want a small, cushion-like plant, trim off these tall shoots low to achieve the desired effect. Whichever way it is treated, Sweet Dream is a good rose for low edging, for mixed plantings and for use in containers.

Size *60cm/2ft × 60cm/2ft*

Raiser *Fryer U.K. 1988*

Parentage *seedling × [(Anytime × Liverpool Echo) × (New Penny × seedling)]*

Awards *JMMM 1998; Award of Garden Merit, RHS; Rose of the Year 1988*

Slight fragrance

THE TIMES *Page 77*

Synonyms KORpeahn; Mariandel, Carl Philip Kristian IV

Winner of many international awards, this fine rose was named in the United Kingdom to celebrate the two hundredth anniversary of the founding of the great London newspaper. The rosette flowers, borne in well-shaped clusters, are of glowing crimson-scarlet with deeper shades within the unfolding petals. Both blooms and foliage have good weather resistance. The juvenile foliage is tinged red and matures into darkest green which retains a purplish, almost black hue. This excellent bedding variety can also be used to make a low-growing hedge.

Size *60cm/2ft × 75cm/2ft 6in*

Raiser *Kordes Germany 1986*

Parentage *Tornado × Redgold*

Awards *PIT, RNRS 1982; Golden Rose of the Hague 1990; Certificate of Merit, Belfast*

Slight fragrance

TRUMPETER *Page 73*

Synonym MACtru

The name of this rose celebrates the great jazz trumpeter Louis Armstrong after whom the parent plant was also named (Satchmo). The brilliant glowing scarlet blooms are carried in large, heavy trusses, on a bushy, almost spreading plant of low to medium growth. This fine bedding variety requires planting towards the front of a mixed bed where its colour would contrast beautifully with blue-flowered perennials.

Blooming from early summer till the first autumnal frost, Trumpeter is of tremendous value in the garden.

Size *60cm/2ft × 60cm/2ft*

Raiser *McGredy New Zealand 1977*

Parentage *Satchmo × seedling*

Awards *Star of the South Pacific, New Zealand 1977; TGC, RNRS; JMMM 1991; Award of Garden Merit, RHS*

Slight fragrance

climbing roses

SUNRISE

Can be grown as a restrained
climber or a wide-arching shrub.

WARM WELCOME

Blooms of unusual brilliance (shown here one and a half times
their actual size) show up well against the bronze-red foliage.

NICE DAY

The sweetly fragrant blooms are perfectly shaped.

COMPASSION

One of the best Modern Climbing
roses, vigorous and sweetly scented.

MADAME ALFRED CARRIÈRE

Now into its second century and still one of the most popular varieties of Climber.

SWAN LAKE

Particularly beautiful on late autumnal evenings.

DREAMING SPIRES
The golden-yellow, semi-double
large blooms are very fragrant.

JOSEPH'S COAT
Can be grown equally well as a
Climber or a Shrub rose.

SUMMER WINE

A vigorous grower whose blooms are of
a glorious colour and sweetly scented.

LAURA FORD

The neatness of the bloom is echoed in the formation of the cluster.

MERMAID

A famous Old rose with single blooms, combining great vigour and elegance.

ALTISSIMO

Single, saucer-shaped blooms appeal to all lovers of single roses.

TRADITION

A vigorous Climber to replace the old red Ramblers
on walls, fences, trellis, pergolas and tall pillars.

DANSE DU FEU

A popular Climber dating from the middle of last
century, it will tolerate being planted in semi-shade.

AGATHA CHRISTIE

Can be treated as a Climber or a loose-growing
Shrub, with large, cup-shaped soft pink blooms.

PENNY LANE

An elegant new Climber that is likely
to be with us for many years to come.

GRAND HOTEL

Blooms throughout summer and autumn with
double crimson flowers and bronze-red foliage.

LITTLE RAMBLER

Large clusters of bloom (over twice the size shown here) smother the shrub-like growth of this choice variety.

HANDEL

A neat *boutonnière* of a rose in white and deep pink.

climbing roses

In the early part of the twentieth century most Climbing roses were the result of mutations from bush or bedding forms of rose. They were described under such names as Climbing Crimson Glory, that is, a climbing form of the bush rose Crimson Glory. In addition, up until a few years ago most climbers bloomed for a matter of a few weeks only, from early to midsummer. The lax-growing Ramblers, an inheritance from the late eighteenth century, bloomed madly for even less time – two to three weeks – and then became a mass of new growth to provide bloom in the following summer. A few Ramblers which still exist may even find a place in the smaller garden.

There were, in addition, some climbing varieties which did not come into either of these categories, having been repeat-flowering climbers from their seedling stages. A few of them survive, including one or two varieties illustrated on the following pages. Today's catalogues and garden centres still offer a few of the once-only flowering varieties but, on the whole, the Climbing roses currently being introduced belong to the repeat-flowering category which, flowering as they do on the current year's growth, require almost no pruning to produce their magnificent crops of bloom.

The recently developed patio climbers, or climbing Miniatures, are tailor-made for the smaller garden, where space can easily be found for them. Raised in the U.K. in the 1980s and 1990s by Chris Warner, they represent one of the major breakthroughs in modern rose breeding. The blooms, in scale with the size of the plant and its foliage, are borne in clusters and, most valuable of all, they flower from top to toe: it is rare to find a patio climber without bloom from early summer until late autumn. Used to fill the small spaces on walls of restricted size, they grow to 90cm/3ft across and up to 2.5m/8ft tall. They may also be planted in large urns or tubs, on pillars and pergolas as well as being grown in small beds as self-supporting shrubs.

AGATHA CHRISTIE *Page 102*

Synonyms KORmeita; Ramira

Named for the famous British crime and mystery writer in 1990, the centenary of her birth, this is a vigorous grower to about 2.5m/8ft, with heavy mid-green glossy foliage. The large, soft pink Hybrid Tea-shaped buds open to full, fragrant cupped blooms almost continuously from early summer to late autumn. The plant rejuvenates itself with much new growth from the base, when mature stems may be removed before they age and become unsightly.

A useful Climber to grow fan shaped on walls of most aspects, or on obelisks and pillars, it will make an attractive, rather loose-growing specimen shrub.

Size *2.5–3m/8–10ft*
Raiser *Kordes Germany 1990*
Fragrant

ALTISSIMO *Page 100*

Synonyms DELmur; Altus; Sublimely Single

A rose for the aficionado of single blooms. The dark crimson Hybrid Tea-shaped buds open to rich crimson-scarlet saucer-shaped blooms, revealing rich golden stamens.

The stiff, upright branches can reach 4m/12ft in height but are best trained into a fan shape to ensure that the blooms are produced all along the horizontal branches.

Altissimo can also be grown as a vigorous upright shrub by shortening the main stems to form the height and outline desired. This will then produce many lateral shoots carrying in wide clusters its blooms of great beauty.

Size *3–4m/10–12ft*
Raiser *Delbard-Chabert France 1966*
Parentage *Tenor x seedling*
Award *Award of Garden Merit, RHS*
Slight fragrance

COMPASSION *Page 94*

Synonym Belle de Londres

One of the greatest of modern Climbers, and the recipient of many awards. Large Hybid Tea-shaped, sweetly scented blooms of soft salmon-pink, often with apricot-buff shadings, are borne singly or in clusters.

The perfect choice for the small garden with room for only one Climbing rose, whether it be fan-shaped on a wall or fence, grown up a pillar or obelisk, or trained on a pergola. It blooms for a long season – flowers have even been gathered on Christmas Day, in midwinter.

Size *2.5–3m/8–10ft*
Raiser *Harkness U.K. 1973*
Parentage *White Cockade x Prima Ballerina*
Awards *HE Medal for fragrance 1973; Gold Medal Baden-Baden 1975; Gold Medal Geneva 1975; Award of Garden Merit, RHS*
Very fragrant

DANSE DU FEU *Page 101*

Synonyms Spectacular; Mada

One of the first of the Modern repeat-flowering Climbing roses. The oval buds are deepest red, opening to scarlet with orange-red shading before fading to leaden red. The blooms, produced over a long season, are borne in clusters set amid dark bronze-green glossy foliage. This hardy rose tolerates being planted in semi-shade but is prone to blackspot.

Size *2.5–3m/8–10ft*
Raiser *Mallerin France 1953*
Parentage *Paul's Scarlet Climber x seedling*
Fragrant

DREAMING SPIRES *Page 96*

Deep golden buds open to large, semi-double, very fragrant golden-yellow blooms which fade to palest apricot as they age. Heavy dark green foliage clothes the tall, upright grower, which repays being trained into a fan shape by producing a fine crop of blooms all summer and autumn along each branch.

Raised by Robert H. Mattock from a cross between a leggy Bush rose and a vigorous Floribunda. It is named for Oxford, the family home, called 'City of dreaming spires' by the poet Matthew Arnold in his poem, *The Scholar Gipsy*.

Size *4–5m/12–15ft*
Raiser *Mattock U.K. 1973*
Parentage *Buccaneer x Arthur Bell*
Award *Gold Medal Belfast*
Very fragrant

GRAND HOTEL *Page 103*

Synonym MACtel

A fine deep red Climber which continues to bloom throughout the summer and autumn. The double crimson blooms,

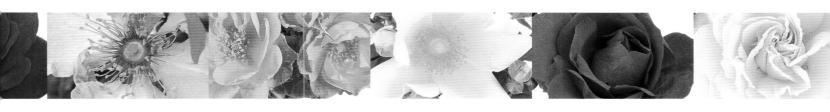

enlivened by lighter shadings, are of good regular cup shape and in well-formed clusters on an upright plant, branching prolifically to make a fine display when trained on a fence. It will tolerate a north-facing aspect, making it a most useful variety. Of average height, Grand Hotel can be kept within bounds to make a neat shrub for the back of a mixed border. The bronze-green foliage is luxuriant.

Size *2.5–3m/8–10ft*
Raiser *McGredy (then) U.K. 1972*
Parentage *Brilliant x Heidelberg*
Slight fragrance

HANDEL *Page 104*

Synonym MACha

The neat, small Hybrid Tea-shaped buds are so good that one often sees them used in buttonholes. The colour can be variable, due to climatic change: strength of sunshine and temperature can both play a part. The buds are creamy white, splashed cherry-pink to red and, as the blooms unfold, the shading spreads across the face of the opening flower, remaining deeper at the frilled petal edge.

An upright grower clothed in dark green foliage, it carries the sprays of bloom continuously throughout the summer and autumn months. Handel is suitable for growing on walls, fences, arches and pillars. It can even be pruned to make an upright, mid-height shrub.

Size *2.5–3m/8–10ft*
Raiser *McGredy (then) U.K. 1965*

Parentage *Columbine x Heidelberg*
Awards *TGC, RNRS; Gold Medal Portland, Oregon 1975; Award of Garden Merit, RHS*
Slight fragrance

JOSEPH'S COAT *Page 96*

A moderate grower which can also be treated as a Shrub rose. Joseph's Coat is, as its name implies, of many colours, showing that the old Floribunda rose Masquerade figures in its ancestry. Shades of golden yellow, orange and red appear on the wide open petals of the semi-double blooms, borne in clusters, which open at different times, accentuating the colour change.

To receive the full benefit from the spread of bloom when grown as a Climber, train each branch as horizontally as possible, having fan-trained the bush from an early age.

Size *2–2.5m/6–8ft*
Raiser *Armstrong and Swim USA 1964*
Parentage *Buccaneer x Circus*
Awards *TGC, RNRS; Gold Medal Bagatelle, France 1964*
Slight fragrance

LAURA FORD *Page 98*

Synonym CHEWarvel

Patio climber. The elegant little buds are like miniature Hybrid Teas and of soft yellow with darker gold shading, deepening as the opening flowers mature. The neatness of the bloom is reflected in the formation of the clusters which can

hold from five to ten blooms, and the plentiful, disease-resistant light green foliage. An excellent choice to grow on a pillar or fan-trained on trellis.

The size of the flower, the foliage and the neatness and weather resistance of the blooms make this, the first of Chris Warner's patio climbers, a fine variety which will tolerate most aspects.

Size *2.5–3m/8–10ft*
Raiser *Warner U.K. 1989*
Parentage *(Anna Ford x Elizabeth of Glamis) x (Galway Bay x Sutter's Gold)*
Awards *Certificate of Merit, RNRS 1988; Award of Garden Merit, RHS*
Fragrant

LITTLE RAMBLER *Page 104*

Synonyms CHEWramb; Baby Rambler

Patio climber. Tiny globular buds of palest rose-pink open to reveal rosette-shaped flowers, packed with petals. Very large clusters of bloom smother this shrubby grower whose pliant main stems can easily grow up to 2m/6ft on a mature plant.

The plentiful, disease-resistant glossy dark green foliage is in perfect scale with the size of the bloom. With its superb fragrance, this is an all-round choice variety for the smaller garden.

Size *2m/6ft*
Raiser *Warner U.K. 1995*
Parentage *(Cécile Brunner x Baby Faurax) x (Marjorie Fair x Nozomi)*
Very fragrant

MADAME ALFRED CARRIÈRE *Page 95*

One of the few Noisette roses still grown, it was described in 1908 as 'the best white Climber'. A large, vigorous grower, it can reach some 6m/20ft and needs a lot of space both vertically and horizontally when grown on a wall; its thin, flexible shoots can, however, be trained easily over a pergola or fence.

The pale green, rather lightweight foliage is plentiful as are the number of pale shoots, giving the undeserved impression of a weak grower, even though it is really vigorous and will tolerate the dappled shade of a northerly aspect. The full, globular blooms are pale creamy white with a hint of palest pink and with gold at the petal base, creating a pearl-like glow. They have the Tea fragrance of many older roses.

Size *up to 6m/20ft*
Raiser *Schwartz France 1879*
Award *Award of Garden Merit, RHS 1993*
Delightful Tea fragrance

MERMAID *Page 99*

A famous Old rose which will need careful siting in the smaller garden as it can grow to 6m/20ft and more – but it can be cut back whenever it seems to be getting out of control. It is included here because there are many gardeners who feel that they must have the charm of Mermaid's single blooms and will create a space for it if they possibly can. These fragrant, 12–15cm/5–6in, sulphur-yellow flowers open flat to reveal a tuft of stamens which remain an attraction even after the petals have fallen.

Mermaid has huge, hooked thorns ready to catch the unwary passer-by – yet another reason for careful siting. The unique glossy foliage is another of this variety's characteristics.

Although recommended as tolerant of a northerly aspect, Mermaid may be cut back by extreme cold (though it will soon recover, as it is a robust grower). This late starter makes up for its tardiness by blooming well into the late autumn.

Size *up to 6m/20ft*
Raiser *Paul U.K. 1918*
Parentage *R. bracteata* x *yellow Tea rose*
Awards *Gold Medal RNRS 1917; Award of Garden Merit, RHS 1993*
Very fragrant

NICE DAY *Page 93*

Synonym CHEWsea

Patio climber. One of the most delightful of the small-flowered climbing Miniatures. The perfect form of the glowing salmon-pink blooms is greatly enhanced by a sweet fragrance. Borne in large, shapely clusters through summer and autumn, the colour of the blooms may lose its brilliance if the plant is grown in the full glare of hot sun, but it is an obvious choice for dappled shade where the bloom and their colour will last longer.

The glossy mid-green foliage is lightly tinted copper-red when young and sets off the bloom in a particularly beautiful manner. The young plant may be shrubby but will mature into a true Climber, well worth waiting for.

Size *2–2.5m/6–8ft*
Raiser *Warner U.K. 1992*
Parentage *Seaspray* x *Warm Welcome*
Very fragrant

PENNY LANE *Page 103*

Synonym HARdwell

The palest pearl-blush or Champagne-coloured blooms, while being most elegantly modern in shape and prolificacy, retain the charm of the Old rose varieties seen in flower paintings.

The delicate shades of soft pink found deep within the unfolding petals of the bloom are beautifully set off by the glossy, dark green foliage. Borne sometimes in wide clusters and at other times singly, the blooms are superb for cutting as they have the substance to last.

Having slightly pliant stems, the plant is vigorous and, although it has not been commercially available for more than a season or two, has already found many admirers. It will tolerate dappled shade and is ideal for walls, fences, pergolas, arches and pillars.

Size *2.5–3m/8–10ft*
Raiser *Harkness U.K. 1998*
Parentage *New Dawn* x *seedling*
Fragrant

SUMMER WINE Page 97

Synonym KORizont

A superb Climber in glowing coral and salmon-pink shades. The semi-double flowers open to reveal a boss of red stamens each tipped with golden anthers. As the bloom develops, the golden-orange reflections fade, leaving the salmon-pink shades which are delightful in themselves. However, if the original fresh colour is desired in a floral arrangement, cut the spray in tight bud and allow it to open indoors, when they will hold both shape and colour well. Summer Wine blooms well into the autumn if dead-headed but, if the last blooms of summer are left, the hips will colour well and remain into the winter.

The vigorous grower is pliant enough to train in a fan shape or round pillars and obelisks. It is excellent for growing on large arches and tall tripods where the blooms' perfume is an added attraction.

Size *4–5m/13–16ft*
Raiser *Kordes Germany 1984*
Awards *TGC, RNRS; Award of Garden Merit, RHS*
Very fragrant

SUNRISE Page 91

Synonyms KORmarter; Freisinger Morgenrote, Morgenrote

The mid-sized double blooms are borne in clusters on plants of moderate growth. It is grown in the raiser's display garden as a wide-spreading Shrub with arching sprays of spectacular proportions.

The soft orange blooms, heavily shaded copper-red, are sweetly scented. There are few good Climbers of this colour, which explains its popularity. In the smaller garden it will find a place growing on low walls, over arches and pillars. Bronze-green, plentiful foliage.

Size *2.5m/8ft*
Raiser *Kordes Germany 1994*
Parentage *Lichkonigen Lucia x seedling*
Sweetly fragrant

SWAN LAKE Page 95

Synonyms MACmed, Schwanensee

Large, fragrant, well-shaped blooms of silvery pale pink are borne in clusters on long stems, making this a dual-purpose variety. It climbs well on walls of most aspects, is good on pillars, arches and obelisks, and the long stems allow for cutting where the blooms are long lasting. It is most attractive in the autumn when the pale, ghost-like blooms are seen at their best in late afternoon.

Size *2–2.5m/6–8ft*
Raiser *McGredy (then) U.K. 1968*
Parentage *Memoriam x Heidelberg*
Fragrant

TRADITION Page 100

Synonyms KORkeltin; Tradition 95

A vigorous Climber with pliable growths, Tradition can be grown in place of the once-flowering red Ramblers. The crimson-scarlet semi-double blooms are borne in enormous clusters throughout the summer and autumn. Most prolific, Tradition can be used to great effect on walls of all sizes, on fences, where it may be trained horizontally, on pergolas as well as to clothe small buildings with its pliant growths. Tradition may be trimmed to shape, though it requires little or no pruning to promote re-growth and more bloom.

Size *4–5m/13–16ft*
Raiser *Kordes Germany 1995*
Fragrant

WARM WELCOME Page 92

Synonym CHEWizz

Patio climber. Warm Welcome is unique among the climbing Miniatures. Its fragrant, semi-double blooms are borne in clusters which clothe the plant from top to toe. Tangerine-orange with orange-vermilion shadings, they have a golden zone at the base of each petal, enhancing the boss of stamens. The bronze-red juvenile foliage ages to deep green and is a perfect foil to the spectacular flowers borne on stems of deep plum-purple. The tall upright plant makes a superb pillar rose as well as being ideal to train on walls, fences and arches.

Size *2.5–3m/8–10ft*
Raiser *Warner U.K. 1992*
Parentage *Elizabeth of Glamis x [(Galway Bay x Sutter's Gold) x Anna Ford]*
Awards *PIT, RNRS 1988; Award of Garden Merit, RHS*
Fragrant

ground cover

WHITE FLOWER CARPET
One of today's most attractive white bedding roses.

FLOWER CARPET (PINK)

The disease resistance of this rose has earned it international acclaim.

ST. TIGGYWINKLE

A vigorous Ground Cover rose whose light pink
blooms are set off by glossy, bright green foliage.

PLAYTIME

The foliage and five-petalled single flowers
proclaim its *Rosa rugosa* ancestry.

KENT

The clusters of well-shaped, weather-resistant white flowers (shown five times their actual size) smother the plant entirely.

GWENT

A fine yellow County Series
rose with spreading growth
(shown here twice its real size).

SURREY

The best known of the County roses
and one of the most versatile (shown
here four times its actual size).

BERKSHIRE

A wide-spreading shrub amply clothed in shiny foliage (shown here at half its actual size).

THE FAIRY

This spreading, bushy grower
(shown nearly twice its actual
size) is an old favourite.

WILTSHIRE

Remains a mass of colour even after the first frosts of autumn.

LANCASHIRE

An exceptional ground-hugging plant in a rich, strong colour.

OXFORDSHIRE

A robust grower, covering
the ground while
remaining very bushy.

ground cover

At one time some of the Shrub roses with a creeping, more sprawling habit were described as 'ground cover roses' and these wide-spreading varieties, many of which had *Rosa wichurana* in their ancestry, were commonly used to carpet the ground in roadside plantings and park landscaping. Unfortunately most of them had inherited the once-only short season of flowering. The newer ground-hugging cultivars to which plant breeders turned their keen interest started to arrive only in the latter half of the twentieth century.

What makes these Ground Cover varieties such an asset to the smaller garden is that they grow to about 90cm/3ft or so wide and they flower right through the season, from early summer until the autumn frosts bring the season to a close. Many of these roses are marketed in groups, such as the County Series, with Surrey appearing in 1988, followed in the 1990s by the Flower Carpet series, launched with a huge marketing campaign in Australia and Europe.

Ground Cover varieties make excellent subjects for borders and bedding and are very useful on banks, particularly where the ground is too steep for planting the more upright-growing roses. These roses also make excellent subjects for large planters and containers, where their spreading growth hangs over and softens the hard edges. The more prostrate varieties have also been used to great effect in hanging baskets, planting three or four plants in a basket of 30–35cm/12–15in in diameter. Given careful cultivation – watering daily in the height of summer and adding a high-potash liquid feed weekly – a hanging basket of roses will last for two or three seasons before needing to be renewed.

BERKSHIRE *page 116*

Synonyms KORpinka; Sommermarchen, Pink Sensation, Summer Fairy Tales, Xenia

A wide-spreading variety becoming ever more popular as time goes by, hence the multitude of different names, which indicate that it is widely grown in many countries.

The large cluster of fragrant, well-shaped blooms open flat, as the brilliant deep cherry-pink petals unfurl to reveal a prominent golden boss of stamens. They are borne on long, arching stems clothed in glossy dark green foliage which is exceptionally disease resistant.

One of the first Ground Cover roses to bloom, it creates a blaze of rich colour throughout the duration of the rose season. A truly excellent variety.

Size *120cm/4ft x 60cm/2ft*
Raiser *Kordes Germany 1993*
Parentage *Weisse Immensee (Grouse) x seedling*
Awards *TGC, RNRS; Gold Medal Glasgow; Gold Medal Baden Baden; Gold Medal Geneva*
Fragrant

THE FAIRY *page 117*

Synonyms Fairy, Feerie

An attractive variety even when not in flower, which is useful because its season starts a few weeks after most other varieties. However, once it starts to bloom this delightful rose is smothered by layer upon layer of clusters of tiny rosette-shaped flowers of soft rose-pink.

As with most repeat-flowering shrubs, The Fairy can be kept within bounds and in shape by judicious pruning, which makes it suitable for many uses in the garden: as ground cover, as a hedge planted to tumble over a low bank or retaining wall, to fill a bed on a terrace, or as a subject for a large planter. It also makes a spectacular weeping standard.

Size *120cm/4ft x 90cm/3ft*
Raiser *Bentall U.K. 1932*
Awards *Award of Garden Merit, RHS*
Little or no fragrance

FLOWER CARPET *page 112*

Synonyms NOAtraum; Blooming Carpet, Emera, Enera Pavement, Heidetraum, Pink Flower Carpet

A good Ground Cover rose which has had many extravagant claims made for it. The colour is a slightly crude, hard pink and it blooms rather later than most of this type. However it does not need dead-heading, seeming indeed to thrive on neglect on this count. The leathery, dark green foliage is as disease-resistant as that of any rose can be, given the conditions under which it may find itself growing.

Size *90cm/3ft x 60cm/2ft*
Raiser *Noack Germany 1989*
Parentage *Immensee (Partridge) x Amanda*
Awards *Gold Medal Glasgow; Award of Garden Merit, RHS; TGC, RNRS*
Slightly fragrant

GWENT *page 115*

Synonyms POULurt; Aspen, Gold Magic Carpet, Sun Cover

The cup-shaped double blooms are bright yellow when they first unfold, later becoming a soft cream, making an almost two-coloured effect in maturity.

The spreading bush is less invasive than some of the Ground Cover varieties and it is well covered in dark green leathery foliage. It has been used to great effect in hanging baskets. Named in Britain to celebrate holding the 1992 National Garden Festival in Ebbw Vale, Gwent, U.K., thus joining the County Series group.

Size *90cm/3ft x 45cm/18in*
Raiser *Poulsen Denmark 1992*
Slight fragrance

KENT *page 114*

Synonyms POULcov; Pyrenees, Sparkler, White Cover

Kent is one of the most useful ground-cover plants. It has been described as a dwarf spreading shrub, as a bedding Floribunda and as Ground Cover. Whichever classification you choose to place it under, a multitude of uses can be found for it. As a small shrub it makes a handsome specimen among dwarf shrubs or as a highlight in bedding. As a bedding rose it is superb planted en masse. In the smaller garden it can in fact be successful anywhere, even grown as a low hedge.

The large clusters of pure white semi-double flowers are well-shaped, fitting nicely into the shrub's low rounded outline. The flowers are most weather resistant and at the height of the season smother the plant to such an extent that little is seen of the foliage. Kent maintains this covering of blooms continuously, making it an excellent plant for every garden.

Size *75cm/2ft 6in x 75cm/2ft 6in*
Raiser *Poulsen Denmark 1988*
Awards *PIT, RNRS 1990; Gold Medal Baden Baden 1990; British Rose Award 1998*
Light fragrance

LANCASHIRE *Page 118*
Synonym KORstesgli

As to be expected, the name Lancashire must apply to a red rose, though in appearance it is quite different from that chosen by the House of Lancaster as its emblem during the English Wars of the Roses. A real ground-hugging variety, the cherry-red double blooms are borne in shapely clusters in quick succession through summer and autumn.

One of the County Series, Lancashire makes an excellent low-spreading ground cover. Its habit of growth also makes it a suitable container plant for trailing over the edge of large planters as well as a good subject for hanging baskets. It makes a spectacular weeping standard too, flowering all through the season.

Size *90cm/3ft x 60cm/2ft*
Raiser *Kordes Germany 1998*

OXFORDSHIRE *Page 119*
Synonyms KORfullwind; Sommermorgen, Baby Blanket, Summer Morning

One of the best of the famous strain from Kordes of Germany, and winner of three well-deserved Gold Medals. The cup-shaped blooms of pale pink are borne in clusters on a vigorously bushy plant. Many of the petals show a likeness to others of the County Series, with frilled edges.

This superb ground-hugging variety is one of the most vigorous, clothed in bright green disease-resistant foliage.

Size *150cm/5ft x 60cm/2ft*
Raiser *Kordes Germany 1991*
Awards *Gold Medal RNRS 1993; Gold Medal Coutrai; Gold Medal Monza*
Parentage *Surrey x seedling*
Lightly scented

PLAYTIME *Page 113*
Synonyms KORsaku; Roselina

A Ground Cover rose with a difference: the foliage, its prickles and the look of the bloom all proclaim its *Rosa rugosa* origins. Unlike so many of the R. *rugosa* hybrids, however, it does not bear hips but as a result flowers on and on. The single rose-pink five-petalled blooms are carried in clusters on a tough and healthy bush which quickly forms a thicket, making it a superb plant for use

in gardens of all sizes.

Size *90cm/3ft x 90cm/3ft*
Raiser *Kordes Germany 1995*
Awards *TGC, RNRS; Crystal Prize Belfast 1995*

ST. TIGGYWINKLE *Page 113*
Synonyms KORbasren; Pink Bassimo

Another very vigorous Ground Cover rose whose fresh, light pink blooms have a prominent white centre, accentuating the boss of golden stamens. The blooms are borne in clusters continuously throughout the summer and autumn and are beautifully set off by the luxurious glossy bright green foliage.

The name originates from the character in the children's book by Beatrix Potter whose illustrations are long-time nursery favourites. This ground-hugging shrub is an excellent subject for the smaller garden.

Size *120cm/4ft x 90cm/3ft*
Raiser *Kordes Germany 1998*
Parentage R. wichurana *seedling x Robin Redbreast*
Awards *Gold Medal 1992*
Light fragrance

SURREY *Page 115*
Synonyms KORlanum; Sommerwind, Vent d'Été

Rather taller than most of the famous County Series of ground-covering roses, Surrey is probably the most popular. It is an excellent choice for planting in

large drifts in beds and borders as well as for growing as specimen plants in smaller sites and in mixed shrub or herbaceous borders.

The soft pink, double cup-shaped blooms develop an attractive frilled edge as they unfurl and present a mass of pink, borne, as they are, in large trusses throughout the summer and autumn.

Growing into a tall (if unpruned) and wide ground-hugging shrub, Surrey also makes a spectacular hedge, but it would need careful siting in the smaller garden where it could easily dominate.

Size *120cm/4ft* x *90cm/3ft*
Raiser *Kordes Germany 1988*
Parentage *The Fairy x seedling*
Awards *Gold Medal, RNRS 1987*
Slight fragrance

WILTSHIRE *Page 118*

Synonym KORmuse

One of the longest flowering of the popular County Series. The spreading ground-hugging shrubs are a mass of bright pink even after the first frosts of autumn have decimated the colour in the rest of the garden.

The semi-double blooms are borne in clusters and, because of continual re-growth, may give a layered effect as the new blooms overtake the maturing ones. The growth is sufficiently lax to make Wiltshire an ideal subject to grow where it can fall over a retaining wall or the edge of a large planter.

Size *90cm/3ft* x *60cm/2ft*
Raiser *Kordes Germany 1993*
Parentage *Partridge x seedling*
Awards *Certificate of Merit, RNRS; Certificate of Commendation, Glasgow*
Some fragrance

WHITE FLOWER CARPET

Page 111

Synonyms NOAschnee; Emera Blanc, Opalia, Schneeflocke

One of the most attractive and popular low-growing white bedding roses available, on account of its neat, compact, ground-hugging habit. When fully established, the clusters of bloom can reach spectacular size and shape. The pure white blooms, large for the size of the bush, are saucer-shaped when mature, revealing the stamens in a very pretty manner.

The compactness of the bush makes this an ideal variety to plant in small terrace beds and in containers, besides its obvious use in mass planting. The dark green, very glossy foliage adds to its attractions.

Size *60cm/2ft* x *60cm/2ft*
Raiser *Noack Germany 1991*
Parentage *Immensee x Margaret Merrill*
Awards *Gold Medal, RNRS; Golden Rose of the Hague 1995; Certificate of Merit, Glasgow 1996*
Fragrant

shrub roses

CORNELIA

One of the most popular Hybrid Musk roses raised in the 1920s by the Reverend J. Pemberton (shown here three times actual size).

CÉCILE BRUNNER

The 'sweetheart rose' is a dainty jewel, half the size shown here.

GOLDEN WINGS

Thought by many to be the most beautiful single rose.

TUMBLING WATERS

A small, spreading, sweetly scented shrub ideal for a container on a terrace.

DE RESCHT

A fine Portland rose brought
back from Persia in the 1930s.

BALLERINA

Has large, rounded clusters of dainty dancing
blooms, almost twice the size shown.

FRAU DAGMAR
HASTRUP

A compact-growing
hybrid of *Rosa rugosa*,
with attractive hips.

JACQUES CARTIER

Brings the charm of the Old Rose garden
into the contemporary small space.

KORDES' ROBUSTA

Vigorous, thorny and repeat flowering,
Robusta makes
a good boundary
hedge.

shrub roses

Found under the headings of Old Garden roses, Species roses and Modern Shrub roses, we find a bewildering array of rose varieties. Differentiated from bedding roses more by their habit of growth than by their breeding, Shrub roses may be defined as roses whose shape and outline allow them to be used as specimen plants, not necessarily to grow among other subjects. They flower from quite low down on the plant, so that when viewed from the side – as opposed to looking down on the bloom, as with bedding roses – they appear to be covered in bloom from the ground upwards.

Not all Shrub roses will fit into small gardens, but those shown here and elsewhere in the book can be accommodated in modest schemes where their repeat-flowering characteristic and their more restrained habit make them a decided asset. These Shrub roses, which may be loosely defined as rose bushes while not falling into the classes of bedding rose, can be used in mixed borders or hedges and some may also be available as standards (Tree roses) because of

their neat, compact habit. By careful selection of varieties, even some of the Old roses (Shrub roses from previous centuries) may find a place in our smaller gardens. A few of the shorter-growing Moss roses, while only summer-flowering, could be squeezed in, such as Nuits de Young. If you are aiming for the look of the old-fashioned rose, try some of the surviving Portland roses such as Jacques Cartier and De Rescht. Portlands, with their full blooms and pastel colours, grow to less than 90cm/3ft in height and flower throughout the summer and autumn.

The individual entries make it clear which recognized category of Shrub rose each profiled variety falls into. The new English roses, which also fall into the Shrub category, merit a section of their own and will be found on pages 136–145.

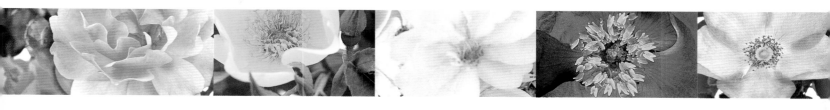

BALLERINA Page 129

The name of this splendid rose describes the dancing single blooms, with each light pink petal edged and shaded with a deeper hue. The flowers, borne in large, rounded clusters, are reminiscent of large-flowered hydrangeas. The elegant shrub is clothed to the ground in plentiful mid-green foliage.

This versatile variety can be used as a specimen on its own, in mixed borders of herbaceous and other plants, or in a Shrub rose border. Ballerina also makes a delightful hedge, blooming with a massive display at the start of the season and thereafter producing colourful sprays of flowers intermittently until another mass of bloom announces the arrival of autumn. Once the last blooms have finished, the shrub is sprinkled with a host of tiny jewel-like hips of bright amber and orange red.

Classification *Modern Shrub rose, repeat flowering*
Size *90cm/3ft* x *90cm/3ft*
Raiser *Bentall U.K. 1937*
Award *Award of Garden Merit, RHS*
Slight fragrance

CÉCILE BRUNNER Page 126

Synonyms Madame Cécile Brunner, Mignon, Sweetheart Rose, Maltese Rose

Perfectly formed, double, fragrant little blooms of china-pink are borne in small sprays carried on almost thornless stems. They are often used in miniature floral arrangements at flower shows.

The dainty, low-growing bush is ideal for the front of a planting whether in a rose bed or a mixed flower border. The foliage is small and, as with most China roses, tinted copper-red when young. This is a famous old variety which has produced a tall, vigorous climbing sport. Care should be taken when purchasing this variety that it is the true small grower: some garden centres may be selling a more vigorous bush with similar flowers (Bloomfield Abundance) erroneously labelled Cécile Brunner.

Classification *China rose, Shrub rose, repeat flowering*
Size *60cm/2ft* x *60cm/2ft*
Raiser *Ducher France 1881*
Award *Award of Garden Merit, RHS*
Sweet fragrance

CORNELIA Page 125

One of the most popular of the Hybrid Musk roses bred in the 1920s by the Reverend Joseph Pemberton. The first was bred from Trier, a white variety with a superb scent from Lambert in Germany. Others of Pemberton's roses include Felicia, Buff Beauty and Penelope, among others no longer listed.

The flowers of Cornelia are borne in sprays on cascading arched branches, which are thornless. The rosette-shaped blooms are of small to medium size, their colour an attractive blend of apricot, salmon, orange and strawberry-pink. The fragrance has been described

as 'musky', referring to the deep sweet perfume which is one of the outstanding attractions of all the Hybrid Musks.

When in full flower, Cornelia is a remarkable beauty, clothed in dark bronze foliage which is lightly tinged red in its juvenile stages.

Classification *Modern Shrub rose, Hybrid Musk*
Size *120cm/4ft* x *120cm/4ft*
Raiser *Pemberton U.K. 1925*
Award *Award of Garden Merit, RHS*
Very fragrant

DE RESCHT Page 128

A small, dense shrub bringing the charm of the Old Garden roses to the smaller garden where its unusual colour and its ability to bloom from early summer to late autumn makes it especially welcome.

The full double blooms are a rounded cushion shape of fuchsia-purple petals surrounding a central button of incurved petals tinted red and purple within the depths of the flower. The compact, rather upright shrub is well furnished with dark green foliage. Overall De Rescht is an easy rose to place for lovers of Old roses with limited space at their disposal.

Classification *Old Garden rose, Portland rose*
Size *Up to 90cm/3ft*
Introduced *into Europe by Miss Nancy Lindsay of Sutton Courtenay, Oxfordshire, from Rasht, Iran in the late 1930s.*
Very fragrant

FRAU DAGMAR HASTRUP

Page 129

Synonyms Fru Dagmar Hastrup, Frau/Fru Dagmar Hartopp

Did Mr Hastrup name his masterpiece after his own wife (or relative) or after Mr Hartopp's wife? The argument goes on but, whatever the story, his rose will live on for many years. It is an excellent variety which will readily find a home in many gardens, large and small. The neat, compact grower of manageable height is smothered in typically heavy wrinkled Rugosa foliage.

The large, soft silvery pink single blooms are produced from late spring until autumn, when they give way to a heavy crop of bright orange and red hips, beloved by birds who will eventually strip the bush. Frau Dagmar makes a superb low hedge and, as with most Rugosas, it will sucker freely. If a budded specimen is planted, the union should be below ground level.

This spectacular shrub is especially delightful when both flowers and fruit are borne at the same time.

Classification *Modern Shrub rose, Rugosa hybrid*

Size *90cm/3ft x 90cm/3ft*

Raiser *Hastrup Denmark 1914*

Awarded *Award of Garden Merit, RHS*

Very fragrant

GOLDEN WINGS *Page 126*

A fine variety from the United States, this five-petalled scented rose of palest lemon-yellow is quite large for a single rose. It opens to reveal dark stamens and, while it looks rather delicate, it is in actual fact both tough and weather resistant. The removal of spent flowerheads will ensure continuity of bloom throughout the summer and autumn.

The vigorous, neat bush is prickly and twiggy after the manner of its briar ancestry and is both hardy and healthy, an ideal variety for the mixed border.

It has been said that the more involved rosarians become with their favourite flower, the more they appreciate the simplicity of the five-petalled rose. Never has this been more true than in the case of Golden Wings.

Classification *Modern Shrub rose, repeat flowering*

Size *120cm/4ft x 120cm/4ft*

Raiser *Shepherd USA 1956*

Parentage *Soeur Thérèse x (Rosa pimpinelifolia Altaica x Ormiston Roy)*

Awards *Gold Medal ARS 1958; Award of Garden Merit, RHS*

Sweet fragrance

JACQUES CARTIER *Page 130*

Synonyms Marchesa Boccella, Marquise Boccella

A fine variety of the Old Garden rose type, sufficiently short and compact to be accommodated in the smaller garden. Of upright habit, the growth is sturdy and the blooms are borne in tight clusters over most of the summer and autumn.

The soft pink blooms are very full and the inner petals are quartered and quilled to produce the shape so popular with the Victorians and which we look for in the Old Rose garden. Their fragrance is superb. The juvenile foliage is light green and develops a bluish tinge as it ages.

This is a great rose to bring the past into our modern small garden; it will make a fine hedge as well as being suitable for the mixed border.

Classification *Old Garden rose, Portland rose*

Size *60cm/2ft x 110cm/3ft 6in*

Raiser *Desprez France 1842*

Very fragrant

KORDES' ROBUSTA *Page 131*

Synonym KORgosa

A vigorous, upright-growing Shrub rose which declares its *Rosa rugosa* ancestry by the mass of thorns which clothe all its stems. The dark, almost blackish crimson slim buds open to large, single bright crimson blooms revealing golden stamens. The well-shaped clusters are of good size and borne freely throughout the summer and autumn.

Of an open habit, Kordes' Robusta can grow quite tall and makes an excellent boundary hedge if pruned lightly, bearing in mind its thorniness.

If pruned hard it will remain a bush of medium height. The foliage is glossy dark green.

Classification *Modern Shrub rose, repeat flowering*

Size *2–2.5m/6–8ft*

Raiser *Kordes Germany 1979*

Parentage *Rosa rugosa × seedling*

Award *Certificate of Merit, RNRS 1980*

Slight fragrance

TUMBLING WATERS

Page 127

Synonym POULtumb

A low-growing shrub, ideal for the smaller garden. At one time it was considered for classification as a bedding (Floribunda) rose, but it was not prostrate enough to put among the Ground Cover roses, despite its name.

The pyramidal spikes of bloom are reminiscent of the *Saxifraga longifolia* hybrid 'Tumbling Waters', from which it gets its varietal name. The semi-double white blooms open flat to expose the golden stamens. The clustered spikes are positioned at all angles, and the cushion-shaped plant is eminently suitable for growing in planters as well as at the front of beds and borders. This Shrub rose also makes an attractive small weeping standard.

Classification *Modern Shrub rose, repeat flowering*

Size *90cm/3ft × 60cm/2ft*

Raiser *Poulsen Denmark 1997*

Sweetly scented

GEOFF HAMILTON

The colour and fragrance of the
cup-shaped quartered blooms
surpass all expectations.

GRAHAM THOMAS

The first blooms in a real yellow, carried in large clusters on slender stems.

MARY ROSE

The large, full flowers borne
in rounded clusters have a
distinct damask fragrance.

THE PILGRIM

One of the most beautiful of the
English roses, its blooms have
curled and infolded small petals.

GOLDEN CELEBRATION

The large, cup-shaped golden-yellow blooms
are a deeper golden-orange in the centre.

EVELYN

The deep, exotic fragrance
of its full, heavy blooms
is enchanting.

english roses

Recent arrivals among the Shrub roses, the new English roses have been bred by David Austin to preserve the outstanding characteristics of the choice Old Garden roses and to give them the obvious virtues of modern hybridization and selection. These English roses are particularly remarkable for their fragrance, from the delicate light fruitiness reminiscent of apples and lemons to the myrrh-like lushness of the old cabbage-rose Hybrid Perpetuals. In appearance, they capture the charm of the old Centifolias and Moss roses as seen in the flower paintings of the Old Dutch Masters, and even the simplicity of the briar rose can be found in these modern masterpieces.

There are many different styles and heights of growth among the English roses, and care should be taken to make sure that the variety you choose is appropriate for your selected site.

ENGLISH GARDEN   *Page 137*

Synonyms AUSbuff; Schloss Glucksburg

Rather less of a shrub than most of the other English Roses from David Austin, English Garden is in appearance more akin to the large-flowered bedding rose. Its shape will therefore blend easily in a traditional bed of Hybrid Teas.

The creamy-buff blooms of beautiful shape open to large, flat flowers shot through with shades of harvest-gold and apricot-pink within the folds of the inner petals. They are ideal for cutting.

Size *60cm/2ft × 90cm/3ft*
Raiser *Austin U.K. 1986*
Parentage *(Lilian Austin × seedling) × (Iceberg × Wife of Bath)*
Fragrant

EVELYN   *Page 142*

Synonym AUSsaucer

The large, full, many-petalled blooms are a beautiful soft tangerine-buff shade, with apricot-pink shading at the heart of the flower. The warmer the weather, the deeper the pink becomes amid the folded and quilled petals. So heavy are these full blooms that the plant may require some support once the otherwise upright stem carrying several at a time causes the branch to arch.

The deep exotic fragrance is so gorgeous that this variety has been adopted by the firm of Crabtree & Evelyn, makers of traditional toiletries and perfume, to promote their products.

Size *75cm/2ft 6in × 90cm/3ft*
Raiser *Austin U.K. 1992*
Parentage *Graham Thomas × Tamora*
Very fragrant

GEOFF HAMILTON   *Page 138*

Synonym AUSham

Round cabbage-shaped buds open to glorious cupped blooms filled with swirls of folded petals. Lovers of Old Garden roses who appreciate how these flowers are portrayed in the old Dutch flower paintings will admire the way the delicately shaded outer petals frame the infolded, quartered blooms of light rose-pink. The fragrance is all that one would expect of an Old rose too. The blooms are borne throughout the summer and autumn on strong, healthy shoots.

This rose is a great tribute to the late Geoff Hamilton, a garden broadcaster on U.K. radio and television who had many admirers.

Size *150cm/5ft × 150cm/5ft*
Raiser *Austin U.K. 1997*
Fragrant

GOLDEN CELEBRATION   *Page 141*

Synonym AUSgold

One of the few varieties with 'gold' or 'golden' in its name that really lives up to its description. The fat buds of golden-yellow open to reveal a centre made up of smaller petals in a deeper orange-golden hue. The large, cup-shaped, very fragrant blooms may become so heavy in wet weather that some support is necessary.

This rounded bush of average size is a good subject for the mixed flower or shrub border, blooming throughout summer and autumn.

Size *90cm/3ft × 90cm/3ft*
Raiser *Austin U.K. 1992*
Parentage *Charles Austin × Abraham Darby*
Very fragrant

GRAHAM THOMAS   *Page 138*

Synonyms AUSmas; English Yellow, Graham Stuart Thomas

The first of David Austin's brilliant English roses in a real yellow. For some years aficionados had enjoyed Austin's pale pink and deep red shades and seen a few roses in orange-buff tints but the advent of Graham Thomas marked a turning point in the series, owing much to the vogue for Old Garden rose lookalikes.

The deep golden buds open to fragrant cup-shaped blooms revealing even deeper golden shades of a quality unusual in a rose, and certainly never before seen in an Old Garden rose. Borne on long, slender stems, the blooms are in large clusters whose weight creates the typical arching habit.

A somewhat leggy plant, it is best planted in groups of three or five to make a clump, or it can be trained to form a restrained climber on walls or tripods by judicious pruning.

Named to honour the rosarian Graham Stuart Thomas who has done much to popularize the revival of the Old Garden rose in Britain and elsewhere.

Size *75cm/2ft 6in x 150cm/5ft*
Raiser *Austin U.K. 1983*
Parentage *Charles Austin x (Iceberg x seedling)*
Award *Award of Garden Merit, RHS 1993*
Fragrant

MARY ROSE *Page 139*

Synonym AUSmary

The large, full flowers with a damask fragrance are borne in rounded clusters on arching branches. The colour of this variety is variously described as 'rich pink' or 'strong rose-pink with a hint of lavender' and even 'mid-pink'. The mature blooms shatter rather than hang on, which saves dead-heading but is of no use to the flower arranger. The round shrub itself is much branched and sturdy, the foliage mid-green and disease resistant.

The rose was named in 1983 to celebrate the great marine archaeological feat of raising from the Solent the 'Mary Rose', the ill-fated flagship of Henry VIII's fleet.

Size *90cm/3ft x 90cm/3ft*
Raiser *Austin U.K. 1983*
Parentage *The Friar x seedling*
Very fragrant

THE PILGRIM *Page 140*

Synonym AUSwalker

This is one of the most beautiful of David Austin's English roses. A multitude of curled and infolded small petals arrange themselves in a most decorative manner in the heart of the quartered, flat bloom. The colour ranges from tints of rich lemon in the centre to the creamy yellow outer petals.

The well-shaped clusters of blooms are held on sturdy stems set amid the luxuriant mid-green foliage. It can be planted to great effect in small groups or even as an individual specimen in a bed or border.

Size *120–150cm/4–5ft*
Raiser *Austin U.K. 1991*
Parentage *Graham Thomas x Yellow Button*
Fragrant

care of roses

Despite the stories that abound about the trouble roses can be, their cultivation is in fact quite simple. It is true that roses need good soil but any soil (except an extremely acidic one, which roses do not like) can be enriched by the addition of rotted organic matter. Many of the ailments that were known to afflict roses, such as blackspot and mildew, are mostly a thing of the past now that disease resistance has been bred into modern varieties. Rose pruning is another task surrounded by myths which have deterred people from growing roses. In fact, trials have shown that a rose blooms as well after it has been drastically 'pruned' by a hedge trimmer as when it has received lighter, more precise treatment with secateurs. Feeding roses is a matter of common sense — a well-fed rose is a healthy plant which will flower well and is better able to resist disease. The essential guidelines to soil, planting, pruning and avoiding pests and diseases are laid out very simply in the following pages.

Soil preparation

'Look over your garden wall with a beautiful rose in your coat, and your neighbour, loitering with his hands in his pockets, knee-deep in groundsel, amid his beds undrained and undug, will sigh from the depths of his divine despair, "What a soil yours is for roses!"'

So wrote S. Reynolds Hole, the Dean of Rochester, in 1901. Dean Hole was one of the founders of the National Rose Society in 1876 (the 'Royal' did not come until the middle of the twentieth century) and is still a name to conjure with in the rose world. His story illustrates a popular belief among gardeners, that roses need exceptional soil, dug three spits deep and frequently enriched with quantities of organic matter, in order to thrive. The truth is that roses will grow in almost any soil except an extremely acidic one and in almost any country in the world. Certainly, if you live in an abnormal weather zone, you will have to carry out extraordinary cultivations but you should not experience difficulties in more temperate zones, provided that the soil is well prepared.

In establishing a garden, it is essential to know what type of soil you have. It would be wonderful if we all had the friable loam rich in nutrients associated with rose culture. However, the use of a good garden compost, composted household waste or farmyard manure is an excellent way of recycling natural materials to build up a healthy soil. It might be that yours is a thin, sandy 'hungry' soil, which will not retain moisture or nutrients, in which case a heavy dressing of farmyard manure, or the addition of well-rotted garden compost, and the use of an organic mulch, will help convert it to a state of fertility.

Your soil may, on the other hand, have the texture of heavy clay, which retains water and certainly makes digging more difficult. In this case you can add organic matter and gypsum or calcified seaweed to lighten the soil and to break down the clay by a process called 'flocculation'. If one of the proprietary preparations or sufficient lime is added to a clay soil, its tiny particles will form much larger 'crumbs', enabling moisture and air to pass through more freely to the benefit of the plant rootlets. Organic manure, compost or any other humus-making materials should be used regularly on all other kinds of soil too, as a matter of routine.

The only soil roses will not grow in is a very acidic soil, such as you find in areas noted for growing rhododendrons, azaleas and winter-flowering heathers. You may come across the term pH factor here, the pH being the measurement of the soil's chemical composition, that is, its degree of acidity or alkalinity. You can buy a soil testing kit from a garden centre if you are unsure of your own soil's chemical composition. If you find that your soil is acidic, you could still grow roses in containers, using a loam-based potting compost.

Having chosen the area of your garden where you wish to plant roses, preparing the soil must be your first

◀ *The addition of organic matter will ensure a healthy rose that blooms well. Here, Climbing rose Madame Alfred Carrière helps to mask an unsightly shed, with hydrangea, euphorbias and peonies.*

▶ *If you find your soil is acidic, you can still grow roses in loam-based potting compost in a container. Standard rose Loving Memory adds depth of colour and becomes the focus of this collection of potted subjects.*

will have a source of good loam. If you have been unable to replace the infected soil, leave it for five years or so before introducing new roses to the same spot. There are preparations on the market which claim to sterilize the soil, enabling one to forego soil replacement but, for a single rose, the effort and expense involved are not really worthwhile, and I have yet to be convinced that the process of chemical soil sterilization is completely effective.

Remember that a rose will last for a number of years, so dig the area well, removing all traces of perennial weeds, and incorporate a liberal dressing of well-rotted garden compost or farmyard manure. How deep you dig may depend on the structure of the soil's surface. Double digging (that is, two spade-depths), where possible, is most effective but if your garden topsoil is only a single spade's depth, then that is how deep you should dig and manure. On no account should a gravel subsoil be disturbed and mixed in with your topsoil, and digging into heavy clay will only strain your back. Dried manure can easily be purchased in bags from a garden centre, or if you have a source of rotted farmyard manure which has been stacked for at least six months, this is ideal. Horse, cow or pig manure is best; poultry or sheep manure can be rather strong and burn young roots or shoots. Other forms of organic matter, such as mushroom compost or hop manure, should be available at your garden centre, and they should be just as effective.

Finally, before digging the planting hole, it is a good idea to make up a planting mixture to be worked into the soil at the bottom of the hole and sprinkled round the roots of the rose after planting it and before filling the hole with the removed topsoil. Make up this mixture simply by adding two generous handfuls of sterilized bonemeal to a large bucket or a small wheelbarrow load (say, 10 litres/2 gallons) of horticultural peat or one of the many alternatives available. This will help to stimulate vigorous root action and give the rose an excellent start in its new home.

consideration. If the proposed site has been occupied by a rose, or roses, within the last five years, it is imperative that the soil is replaced before planting. Remove at least a wheelbarrow load (say, 60cm/2ft x 60cm/2ft x 60cm/2ft) of 'old' soil and take it to another part of the garden not occupied by roses before replacing it with fresh topsoil. This is because of an almost certain infection known as 'rose sickness' or 'specific rose transplant disease' which is liable to stay in the soil for several years after the removal of old, established roses.

In small plots it is often difficult to find topsoil elsewhere in the garden to replace the old soil with. If you need only a small quantity, a local garden centre will almost certainly sell bags of topsoil, but where a large amount is required, search through a local directory to find a 'turf and soil supplier' who

Planting roses

Marking out a rose bed

First decide the effect you are aiming for, whether formal or informal, and prepare and clear the site. Then obtain a bunch of marking canes (60cm/2ft tall) and a length of cord to mark out a straight planting line. Using the recommended planting distances (see right), work out the planting pattern and stick in a cane where each rose plant is to go. The front row should be parallel to the edge of the bed, leaving a 45cm/18in border. Use the cord line to ensure straight lines if you want a formal bed. Make any necessary adjustments to achieve an overall sense of balance before you start to dig. Ensure that the soil is moist (but not wet) before digging the planting hole.

To plant a Shrub or bedding rose, follow the sequence shown opposite. If you have ordered bare-rooted roses and they arrive at an inconvenient time, or if the weather is too wet or too cold for planting, 'heel' the roses in, temporarily planting them in a trench, where they may be safely kept until conditions improve.

Planting Climbing roses

When planting a climber against a wall or fence, take care to ensure that the site is not excessively dry, which is often the case when the wall is facing the sun. Prepare the ground thoroughly, then dig a planting hole at least 45cm/18in away from the wall, to avoid the driest area at its foot. Make the hole 60cm/2ft square and deep enough to accommodate the roots or the rootball. At the bottom of the hole, incorporate a liberal dressing of organic planting mixture containing sterilized bonemeal and plenty of fibrous matter (see page 149). Place the plant in the hole as for a Shrub rose (see opposite), but with the cane leaning against the wall or fence. Keep the newly planted Climbing rose well watered during the first season after planting. It is also advisable not to grow any other plants any closer to the rose than 60cm/2ft.

Recommended planting distances

When planting new roses, check the ultimate height your plant is expected to reach in maturity. This will give you an indication of the recommended planting distance between like specimens, which should be about two-thirds of that height.

PATIO ROSES		45cm/18in apart
HYBRID TEAS & FLORIBUNDAS		60cm/2ft apart
SHRUB ROSES	Short	90cm/3ft apart
	Medium	1.2m/4ft apart
	Tall	2m/6ft apart
CLIMBING ROSES		2.5m/8ft apart minimum
STANDARD ROSES		1.2m/4ft apart minimum

Newly planted Hybrid Teas and Floribundas should be pruned hard in the first spring after planting, but newly planted Shrub roses and Climbing roses need no pruning in the first year.

Planting a rose hedge

Prepare the site well as for a rose bed (see page 148) and dig a trench along the line of the proposed hedge. The width of the hedge will narrow the choice of variety used. For a neat, upright hedge more than 90cm/3ft tall, a single line of upright (not bushy) Floribundas will be suitable. Should you want a thicker hedge with much the same characteristics, use a staggered line (two lines 15–30cm/6–12in apart, with individual plants at alternate stations and no more than 60cm/2ft between plants) to give the desired effect. Reduce the planting distances given above by at least 10 per cent for a hedge, as your aim is to present an unbroken line of growth.

1. Dig a hole large enough to accommodate the roots of a bare-rooted rose (this will be about the width and depth of the spade) or the rootball of a container-grown plant. At the bottom of the hole, fork up a tilth of loose, friable soil and work in a handful of planting mixture. Spread out the roots evenly in the planting hole

2. Agitate the rose slightly to ensure that it is 'sitting' comfortably in the planting mixture, then add another handful of planting mixture and top up with removed soil, firming as you go. When planted, the point of union between the rootstock and the cultivar should be level with the surface of the soil.

3. Tread the soil round the plant to firm it in. This may need to be repeated after frosty weather and throughout the winter to prevent 'wind rock'. If planting a number of roses in a new bed, it is a good idea to co-ordinate the procedure. After digging the hole and planting the first rose, fill the hole with soil removed from the next site, and so on.

Moving mature roses

It is unlikely that an ancient rose will survive being moved but, if a rose is less than five years old, you may wish to transfer it to a new site – or indeed a new garden – and care must be taken to ensure its survival. To dig out the old plant, first loosen it in the soil by cutting a circle round the base of the rose at a distance of 60–75cm/2ft–2ft 6in. You may need to do this in two stages – the first will loosen the compacted soil and the second time the spade, going in deeper, will sever the wide-spreading roots. Two people working at opposite sides will make the task easier. The soil making the rootball is not important and can be left behind. Once the rose has been removed, prune the roots. Broken and scraped roots can be trimmed back cleanly, using a sharp knife or secateurs. Remove any suckers you see as well as snags of dead wood and trim back very soft young shoots.

Soak the new site thoroughly before planting, especially if the weather has been dry (in which case it is also a good idea to moisten the roots before replanting). Once the wet soil starts to dry out, leaving the surround moist, plant your rose, using a planting mixture such as peat and bonemeal (see page 149). Firm in your replanted rose by treading down the infill with your foot. Keep a close eye on the replanted rose until it is re-established, watering at regular intervals if dry.

Pruning roses

Pruning roses involves the removal of aged, spent or unsightly wood to promote healthy new growth in order to regenerate the plant. The purpose is to enable the rose to produce a good crop of blooms and foliage to grace the garden in the season to follow.

It is worth observing a few basic rules to ensure success. Before starting to prune, tidy up the plant, not only to remove dead or diseased wood, but to make things easier for you at the next stage. Weak or damaged shoots are extremely unlikely to produce good results. Aim to remove crossing shoots too, if possible, so that future growth will ensure that light and air can reach all parts of the plant; this will help to keep the foliage healthy. All cuts made should be finished cleanly, using an ultra-sharp pruning knife or a pair of by-pass secateurs. Your sharp secateurs will leave a clean, hygienic cut without ragged edges and ensure that the wound heals as quickly as possible. Make the cut on a slant, leaving the bud as near to the top of the remaining wood as possible, in order to leave no snags above developing new shoots. Stems should be cut back, leaving two or three buds on the previous year's growth.

Some authorities say that you must prune hard to be kind. Others that if you do so, you are depriving the plant of its reserves by cutting back too far and that you only need to reduce a bedding rose by half to ensure good results. If a variety is tall and vigorous with several thick, healthy stems growing from the base of the plant, these are the shoots which will produce fine blooms and strong, healthy foliage. If you want your garden to be a blaze of colour, with masses of blooms in the early summer, light pruning to a third of last year's growth should produce the desired result. To achieve strong, healthy growth and foliage, together with blooms of good quality, harder pruning of last year's growth is acceptable. Whichever programme you follow, it is essential to take note of the results and take them on board in future pruning regimes.

Pruning bedding roses

Hybrid Tea, Floribunda, patio and Ground Cover roses are all varieties and types that flower on the current year's growth and should be pruned when the plants are dormant, if possible just before growth starts in early spring. If your rose is really old, has been pruned badly in the past and the base of the plant is full of gnarled wood, you may need to carry out a drastic operation by cutting into the old, unsightly wood. Do so when the plant is almost completely dormant, in midwinter. This will ensure that there is no sap rising in the plant and will therefore avoid any 'bleeding' when you cut into it. You may need to use a saw on the gnarled old wood.

▲ *This Rambler rose, swathing the arch, blooms on growth produced in the previous summer. It rejuvenates itself by regrowth from the base of the plant in late summer, so pruning should be carried out in early autumn.*

The growth which has flowered may be cut back hard, leaving the new young growth to be tied in to replace it and to bear blooms the following summer. The form of a well-pruned rose can best be appreciated in winter.

To the nervous gardener this may appear dangerous to the plant but many unsuspected dormant buds will be forced into growth by this drastic action. If such treatment does kill the rose, though it is unlikely, console yourself that the aged plant was no longer an ornament in the garden and you have only hastened the inevitable.

At the end of the growing season, it is a good idea to trim your bedding roses back to a uniform height (say to 60cm/2ft high). This will help to tidy up the garden for the winter and will stop 'wind rock' in the taller specimens. Once this occurs, the roots can be easily damaged by frost or by waterlogging. Early spring pruning is recommended just

before the onset of spring growth, the actual month or week depending on that year's weather pattern and your geographical location. If your roses have started to shoot into growth to about 5–8cm/2–3in, you have left it till just the right time to prune. Do not prune during periods of hard frost. This does not mean that the plant will be damaged by a 'snap' frost the day after pruning, merely that the plant must not be frozen at the actual time of the cut. Iced tissue will bruise badly if touched at that time.

As we have seen under Planting Roses (page 150), newly planted bedding roses must be pruned hard (to about 10cm/4in) in the spring after planting to ensure a good, broad-based framework on which the future of the plant will depend. The roots of your new plant will also be less stressed if they are not subjected to early spring winds.

Pruning Climbing roses

Almost all the recently introduced Climbing rose varieties bloom on the current year's growth. Therefore it does not greatly matter whether you prune hard or not, unless the plant has become top-heavy or if, after a few years, you wish to remove old or unsightly growth.

The main operation to which your Climbing rose needs to be subjected is training (see page 37). In most cases, the aim of training is to ensure that growth and therefore foliage and bloom are borne as close to the ground as possible. Tie all new and recently produced shoots down to an almost horizontal position – which means that you must have something to tie these branches to. Use wooden trellis or fix wires to your wall or fence by means of vine eyes or masonry nails. In training your Climbing rose to a fan shape, you will see which shoots need shortening or removing. There will, of course, be some shoots which remain vertical. If, however, you try to hurry the coverage of the wall by training all shoots straight up, you will finish with a top-heavy plant with stems that are bare to about halfway up.

1. *Newly planted Hybrid Tea and Floribunda roses should be pruned the first spring after planting, before they start to produce shooots.*

2. *Fairly light pruning at this stage will allow your rose to produce some early blooms during its first year.*

3. *Harder pruning at the same stage ensures healthy basal shoots, better foliage and large, shapely blooms in due course.*

In the case of the older, summer-flowering only Climbing roses, the main frame of the plant should be left trained to cover the allotted area, while the lateral growths bearing blooms should each be shortened to two or three buds in the spring.

Ramblers, which also flower on growth made the previous year, need special treatment. They usually bloom profusely in midsummer and spend the rest of the growing season producing new growth from the base of the plant. After they have finished blooming, all of the summer's flowering growth can be removed by pruning and the new basal shoots should be securely tied in to bloom in the following season.

Pruning Shrub roses

Shrub roses also fall into two main categories – those which bloom on the previous year's growth and those which bloom on the current year's growth. The latter can be trimmed or pruned in order to shape the plant to fit the available space. It does not really matter if you cut back these Shrub roses quite hard, as has been shown during trials using a hedge trimmer for pruning – they will still produce bloom in the forthcoming season. They may, however, lose the shape you

have assiduously worked to produce during more considered trimming. On the other hand, they will definitely benefit from a severe prune, while at the same time removing all dead, diseased and straggly growth.

Shrub roses which bloom on the previous year's growth, which applies to most of the Old Garden roses, the Ramblers, the Species roses and just a few of the Modern Shrub roses, would suffer seriously if you cut them hard back and pruning them severely at the wrong time would probably result in no bloom whatever in the following summer. Little or no pruning of the previous year's growth is what is required here; instead, the growths which have bloomed – and this usually means in midsummer, with no repeat in late summer or autumn – can be cut back during the autumn after flowering, providing you leave on enough of the summer's growth for the rose to bloom and enhance your garden the following year.

It is therefore essential to know exactly what roses you have and to which group they belong before embarking on your pruning programme. If you move into a garden that is already stocked with roses and you do not know what type or varieties they are, seek help from a local horticulturalist or garden centre.

1. Standard roses require a certain amount of pruning after they have flowered.

2. Remove any spindly and/or diseased or dead wood before pruning the healthy, vigorous stems to a manageable length. Then stand back and observe – balance is particularly important with standard roses and after pruning you may need to cut a little more to avoid lop-sided growth.

3. Harder pruning will produce better results in the long term, even if this means leaving just two or three buds on the remaining wood.

Pruning standard roses

Many Hybrid Tea and Floribunda varieties are also grown as standard (Tree) roses and they need the selection of strong-growing shoots to encourage a well-balanced head, by means of careful pruning (see above). Standard roses are budded on to rootstocks, with the budding taking place well above ground level. The stems of standards often produce suckers between the ground level and the 'head' of the rose and these should be rubbed off as soon as they appear. Do not allow them to ripen.

Pruning rose hedges

Pruning the roses in a hedge is a little different to their treatment when grown in beds and borders. Especially where space is restricted, pruning needs to be done to achieve an even hedge of appropriate height and width, rather than pruning for maximum flower production. Hybrid Teas and Floribundas should be encouraged to re-grow from the base of the plant each year. If you have not pruned down to a reasonable height, all re-growth will be from the top of the plants and this may be repeated year on year. If this has occurred and you wish to cut into old, gnarled wood, do so while the roses are dormant. Do not leave it until the onset of

spring or the wound will not heal properly and much sap, and therefore vigour, will be lost.

At the end of the flowering season, a hedge may be clipped to a uniform height once you are not expecting any more blooms; by reducing the height, you will avoid wind-rock during winter gales. Do not allow a hedge to reach its intended height in one go – always prune it down to the height of the lowest plant in the hedge in the early years. If your hedge is made up of Shrub roses, it may not need hard pruning, merely trimming to shape. Whether it is squared off or rounded at the edges is a matter of preference. If the Shrub roses are once-flowering Old Garden types, do not cut back young growth; to do so would make your rose hedge stay green throughout the year. Instead, lightly trim any invasive shoots to a manageable length.

Repeat-flowering Shrub roses, that is, varieties which bloom on the current year's growth, may be pruned to suit your requirements. Height may be achieved by light pruning but if the hedge is becoming overcrowded, hard pruning will cause no harm. After a year or so of light pruning, mature Shrub roses, particularly Rugosas, may become bare at the base and will benefit from hard pruning in midwinter to restore them to the production of compact growth.

Feeding roses

The most important part of rose cultivation is to make sure your plants stay healthy by following good gardening practice. An organic approach, which is a way of working with nature rather than against it, is recommended here, and as part of this regime, feeding, mulching and good hygiene all play a crucial part. Healthy plants will flower well and are better able to resist most forms of pest or disease.

There are seven main elements which are essential to plant growth: nitrogen, phosphorus, sulphur, potassium, calcium, magnesium and iron, in addition to what are commonly known as trace elements. An analysis of your soil should show up any particular deficiency. Organic fertilizers or feed (as opposed to inorganic chemicals) are readily available at garden centres or shops. One of the best compound feeds is a mixture of blood, fish and bonemeal: fishmeal contains nitrogen and phosphates; bonemeal contains phosphate fertilizers for activating root action; and dried blood contains fast-acting nitrogen. Scatter a small handful around each rose as soon as the first leaves appear in the spring, and repeat this at the height of the main flowering. This second application should keep the plant in good health for the rest of the season. Alternatives include hoof and horn, a good source of slow-release nitrogen; seaweed, which includes a complete range of trace elements; and dried animal manures, which are rich in humus-building nutrients.

It is also a good idea to spread an organic mulch, such as pulverized tree bark, around your roses to retain moisture in the soil. Not only will it smother annual weeds but it will aid the roses' assimilation of plant foods, even at the height of summer. Otherwise the soil would dry out, locking up most of the nutrients the rose needs in order to continue to produce strong, healthy growth, foliage and blooms.

▸ *Well-fed Rambling roses* The Garland *(left) and* Dorothy Perkins, *together with* Félicité Perpétue *(right), clothe the garden arches seen here in high summer.*

Keeping roses healthy

▲ *A healthy, well-fed rose should stay free of attack from pests or disease. Climbing rose Bantry Bay, trained up a wigwam of canes, responds with a mass of blooms and shiny green foliage.*

A well-grown and well-nurtured rose will be able to resist pests and diseases, whereas an unhealthy, starved plant will be the first to succumb. Apart from generous feeding (see page 156), there are some aspects of rose cultivation which you should follow to prevent particular problems.

Leaf shedding in midsummer

One of the commonest causes of leaf drop is lack of moisture and sustenance. Feed your roses with a balanced rose food, available from most garden centres, and mulch with organic compost and/or pulverized bark. This will retain moisture in the soil and help the plant roots draw up nutrients.

Lack of late summer blooms

After the midsummer flush, repeat-flowering roses need a little extra cosseting, in the form of mulching and dead-heading, to continue to perform well. The removal of spent blooms will stop seedheads (hips) from forming and taking the nourishment from autumn blooms. This applies to repeat-flowering Hybrid Teas, Floribundas and Climbers. Shrub roses that are prized for their production of ornamental hips should not, of course, be dead-headed. A few Ground Cover roses, particularly those with single flowers, while blooming until the early winter, will also produce colourful hips if not dead-headed in late summer.

Discoloured leaves

The foliage on a strong, healthy, well-nourished rose should be richly coloured and mirror the plant's well-being. Discoloured leaves give the first warning that all is not well. The chart opposite shows symptoms affecting foliage, their diagnosis and recommended treatment. Leaves affected by blackspot should be picked off as soon as they are detected, then burnt, which should stop the attack spreading. Remove and burn all twiggy growths, together with any prunings.

Rose pests and diseases

A number of insect predators, such as ladybirds, attack and eat greenfly (aphids), the most common rose pest, though badly infected plants can also be sprayed with insecticidal soaps. Roses may become infected with fungal diseases in years when these are prevalent. To a great degree, these can be circumvented by keeping your plants strong and healthy through regular feeding and mulching, especially in early and late summer.

Dealing with weeds

The whole range of weed-killing potions, paints and sprays currently on sale at garden centres and hardware stores all carry dire warnings about their misuse, which make it obvious that in the smaller garden the safest and best course of action is prevention. When preparing a new site for planting, it is imperative that all perennial weed roots are dug out and destroyed. Thereafter, mulches make admirable suppressants for annual weeds. The use of pulverized bark, applied in a 5cm/2in layer over the top of the soil in between your roses, will control most annual weeds and the odd weed that escapes these attentions can easily be dealt with by hoeing or by hand weeding.

Symptom	Probable cause	What to do
Yellowing leaves	Lack of available iron (this even occurs in some iron-rich soils – the keyword is 'available')	Apply iron in the form of a proprietary brand of sequestered iron
Yellowing of leaf-tissue around veins	Magnesium deficiency	Water in 25g/¾oz per sq m/sq yd of Epsom Salts
Pale green leaves	Lack of nitrogen	Water in 45g/1½oz of hoof and horn
Small leaves with reddish-purple shading	Lack of phosphorus	Water in 25g/¾oz superphosphate
Red/purple edges to leaves/brilliant red shading on juvenile growth	Lack of potash	Water in 25g/¾oz sulphate of potash
White deposit coating the leaves	Mildew	Spray with a good fungicide, and feed well until midsummer
Round black spots on green leaves (not purple) or on leaves which have turned yellow in autumn	Blackspot	As above, and pick off affected leaves and destroy. Feed well the following spring

A layer of moss or green algae on the soil may point towards poor drainage, causing waterlogging, compaction of the soil or a manurial deficiency. Hoeing, the use of an organic mulch and feeding should take care of a minor problem but serious drainage problems call for more drastic measures, which may involve laying trenches. However, most waterlogging is caused by abnormal weather conditions.

Removing suckers

Most roses are budded on to a rootstock, usually a selection of a briar. At one time most of the briars were a form of dog rose (*Rosa canina*), a vigorous and often invasive wild rose. The vigour of the plant is what the propagator is using to the advantage of the cultivar. Selections of other briars have sometimes been made on various grounds, such as incompatibility or a reduced liability to produce suckers.

Suckers are shoots which grow from the briar rootstock or from just below the bud union of the named variety (cultivar) and the briar. These growths can impede the rose's performance. Tracing the suspect shoot to its origin is often the most reliable way to identify a sucker. An old tale, often repeated through ignorance, is that the number of leaflets on a bract is a sure sign of identity. The truth is that modern varieties are so mixed up in their ancestry that the inherited number of leaflets is immaterial and can vary even on the same plant, so the number of leaflets may be the same on a sucker as on the cultivar. Compare the rogue shoot with the juvenile as well as the mature growth of a budded shoot: if it is the same or similar, it is probably not a sucker.

A rose may be induced to sucker if it has been damaged by hoeing too near the root, or by wrongly hacking off a previous sucker at ground level, leaving a stump to grow again. Planting a new specimen too loosely also encourages suckering. Deal with a sucker as soon as you see it: follow the course of the shoot in question, which may involve moving soil away until you discover its origin. Then pull off the sucker, wearing suitable gloves. If you cut a sucker you may only be pruning it, which encourages renewed vigour.

Roses for special purposes

Although roses fall into various groups based on a worldwide classification, it is often more helpful to see them listed according to their use in the garden. The following lists include all the roses featured in this book (marked with an asterisk*); they are based on, but do not rigorously follow, the lists of Roses of Special Merit published by The Royal National Rose Society, the world authority on roses.

Key to headings and abbreviations:

Name Varietal name used in reference lists

Code International code for identification of variety and raiser (the first three or four letters are those of the breeder's name). Where no code name is given, this rose predated the practice of giving international names.

Height The heights given are for mature plants grown under average conditions of cultivation and under different and/or particular circumstances may vary from the norm.

S short: 45–75cm/18in–2ft 6in M medium: 75–90cm/2ft 6in–3ft

T tall: 90cm/3ft upwards

Fragrance F barely perceptible fragrance, FF fragrant, FFF very fragrant

Climbers W: for walls and fences P: for pillars and obelisks A: for arches and pergolas

ROSES FOR MIXED BEDS AND BORDERS

Name	Code	Height	Type	Colour	Fragrance
Amber Queen	HARroony	S	Fl	Amber/yellow	FF
Anna Livia*	KORmetter	M	Fl	Rose-pink	F
Avon	POULmulti	S	GC	Pale blush	F
Ballerina*		M	Sh	Pale pink	F
Belle Epoque	FRYyaboo	M	HT	Amber/bronze	FF
Berkshire*	KORpinka	M	GC	Cherry-pink	F
Charles Notcutt*	KORhassi	T	Sh	Crimson-scarlet	F
Cleopatra*	KORverpea	T	HT	Scarlet/gold reverse	F
Comte de Chambord		M	Sh	Pink	FFF
Congratulations*	KORlift	T	Fl	Soft pink	F
Cornelia		M	Sh	Pink	FFF
Crystal Palace*	POULrek	S	Pat	Creamy peach	F
Dawn Chorus*	DICquasar	M	HT	Tangerine-orange	FF
De Rescht*		M	Sh	Fuchsia-purple	FFF
Elina	DICjana	T	HT	Primrose-yellow	FF
English Garden*	AUSbuff	T	Sh	Soft apricot-yellow	FF
Evelyn*	AUSsaucer	M	Sh	Apricot	FFF
Fascination*	POULmax	S	Fl	Shrimp-pink	F
Felicia		T	Sh	Shaded pink	FFF
Fellowship*	HARwelcome	M	Fl	Deep orange	F

Name	Code	Height	Type	Colour	Fragrance
Festival*	KORdialo	S	Pat	Crimson-scarlet/silver	F
Flower Carpet*	NOAtrum	M	GC	Deep pink	F
Freedom	DICjem	M	HT	Chrome yellow	F
Geoff Hamilton*	AUSham	M	Sh	Shades of pink	FF
Gertrude Jekyll	AUSbord	T	Sh	Deep pink	FFF
Golden Celebration*	AUSgold	M	Sh	Deep gold	FFF
Golden Wings*		M	Sh	Pale lemon-yellow	FF
Graham Thomas*	AUSmas	T	Sh	Rich yellow	FFF
Gwent*	POULurt	S	GC	Lemon-yellow	F
Hannah Gordon*	KORweiso	M	Fl	Shaded pink	F
Heritage	AUSblush	T	Sh	Shell-pink	FFF
Hertfordshire	KORtenay	S	GC	Carmine-pink	F
Iceberg*	KORbin	T	Fl	White	FF
Ice Cream	KORzuri	M	HT	White shaded ivory	FF
Ingrid Bergman*	POULman	M	HT	Glowing dark red	FF
Intrigue*	KORlech	M	Fl	Deepest crimson	F
Irish Eyes	DICwitness	S	Fl	Yellow and scarlet	F
Jacques Cartier*		S	Sh	Warm pink	FFF
Just Joey*		M	HT	Apricot-buff	FF
Kent*	POULcov	S	GC	White	F
Korresia*	KORresia	M	Fl	Brilliant yellow	FFF
L.D. Braithwaite	AUScrim	T	Sh	Deep crimson	FFF
L'Aimant	HARzola	T	Fl	Coral-pink	FFF
Lancashire*	KORstesgli	S	GC	Crimson	FF
Little Bo-peep	POULlen	S	Pat	Palest pink	F
Mandarin*	KORcelin	S	Pat	Orange and pink	F
Many Happy Returns	HARwanted	M	Fl	Silvery pink	F
Mary Rose*	AUSmary	T	Sh	Rose-pink	FFF
Molineux	AUSmol	T	Sh	Rich yellow	FFF
Oranges and Lemons*	MACanlorem	T	Fl	Yellow striped orange	F
Oxfordshire*	KORfullwind	M	GC	Soft pink	F
Paul Shirville	HARqueterwife	M	HT	Peach, salmon shading	FFF
Peace*		T	HT	Yellow, pink shading	F
Playtime*	KORsaku	M	GC	Pink	F
Queen Mother*	KORquemu	S	Pat	Soft pink	F
Remember Me	COCdestin	M	HT	Coppery orange	F
Royal William*	KORzaun	T	HT	Deep crimson	FF
St. Tiggywinkle*	KORbasren	S	GC	Glowing pink/white eye	F
Sally Holmes		T	Sh	Ivory shaded buff	FF
Selfridges*	KORpriwa	T	HT	Bright yellow	FF

Name	Code	Height	Type	Colour	Fragrance
Sharifa Asma*	AUSreef	M	Sh	Blush-pink	FFF
Shocking Blue*	KORblue	M	Fl	Rich lilac-magenta	FFF
Silver Jubilee*		M	HT	Apricot-salmon	F
Sunset Boulevard*	HARbabble	M	Fl	Orange-apricot	F
Surrey*	KORlanum	M	GC	Soft rose-pink	F
Sweet Dream*	FRYminicot	M	Pat	Creamy apricot	FF
Tequila Sunrise*	DICobey	S	HT	Yellow shaded red	F
The Fairy*		M	GC	Soft rose-pink	
The Pilgrim*	AUSwalker	T	SH	Pale lemon-yellow	FFF
The Times*	KORpeahn	M	Fl	Deep crimson	F
Trumpeter*	MACtru	S	Fl	Glowing scarlet	F
Tumbling Waters*	POULtumb	M	Sh	White	FF
Tynwald*	MATtwyt	T	HT	Ivory-white	FF
Valencia*	KOReklia	T	HT	Buff-orange	FFF
Warm Wishes*	FRYxotic	M	HT	Salmon-peach	F
White Flower Carpet*	NOAschnee	S	GC	White	FF
Wiltshire*	KORmuse	S	GC	Bright rose-pink	F
Winchester Cathedral	AUScat	M	Sh	White	FFF
Worcestershire	KORalon	M	GC	Lemon-yellow	F

ROSES FOR HEDGES

Name	Code	Height	Type	Colour	Fragrance
Alexander	HARlex	T	HT	Scarlet	
Ballerina*		M	Sh	Pale rose-pink	F
Charles Notcutt*	KORhassi	T	Sh	Crimson-scarlet	F
Cornelia		M	Sh	Pink shades	FFF
De Rescht*		S	Sh	Fuchsia-purple	FFF
Frau Dagmar Hastrup*		M	Sh	Silver-pink	FF
Golden Wings*		M	Sh	Pale lemon	FF
Iceberg	KORbin	M	Fl	White	F
Jacqueline du Pré	HARwanna	M	Sh	White	FF
Kent*	POULcov	S	GC/Sh	White	F
Kordes' Robusta*	KORgosa	T	Sh	Crimson	F
Korresia*	KORresia	S	Fl	Bright yellow	FFF
L.D. Braithwaite	AUScrim	M	Sh	Deep crimson	FFF
Little Bo-peep	POULlen	S	Pat	Palest pink	FF
Mary Rose*	AUSmary	M	Sh	Rose-pink	FF
Playtime*	KORsaku	S	GC	Pink	F
Romantic Hedgerose	KORworm	M	Fl	Pink	F
R. glauca*		T	Sh	Rose-pink	F
R. rugosa 'Alba'		M	Sh	White	FFF

Name	Code	Height	Type	Colour	Fragrance
R. rugosa 'Rubra'		M	Sh	Rose-pink	FFF
Surrey*	KORlanum	M	GC	Soft pink	F
The Fairy*		S	GC/Sh	Soft pink	
The Pilgrim*	AUSwalker	M	Sh	Pale lemon	FFF
The Times*	KORpeahn	S	Fl	Rich crimson	F
Winchester Cathedral	AUScat	M	Sh	White	FF

CLIMBING ROSES FOR WALLS AND FENCES, PILLARS, PERGOLAS AND ARCHES

(All roses listed will tolerate a northern or easterly aspect)

Name	Code	Height	Type	Colour	Fragrance
Agatha Christie*	KORmeita	W		Soft pink	FF
Altissimo*	DELmur	WP		Crimson-scarlet	F
Bantry Bay		WPA		Soft pink	F
Compassion*		WPA		Pink shaded apricot	FFF
Danse du Feu*		W		Cinnabar-red	F
Dreaming Spires*		WP		Golden-yellow	FFF
Golden Showers		WPA		Clear yellow	F
Graham Thomas*	AUSmas	WP		Golden-yellow	FFF
Grand Hotel*	MACtel	WPA		Bright crimson	F
Handel*	MACha	WPA		White shaded pink	F
Joseph's Coat*		P		Yellow/orange	F
Laura Ford*	CHEWarvel	WPA		Golden-yellow	FF
Little Rambler*	CHEWramb	PA		Palest pink	FFF
Madame Alfred Carrière*		W		Pearly white	FFF
Mermaid*		W		Primrose-yellow	FF
New Dawn		WPA		Flesh-pink	FF
Nice Day*	CHEWsea	WPA		Salmon-pink	FFF
Open Arms	CHEWpixcel	PA		Light pink	F
Penny Lane*	HARdwell	WPA		Champagne	FF
Summer Wine*	KORizont	WA		Coral-pink	FFF
Sunrise*	KORmarter	PA		Yellow and orange	FFF
Swan Lake*	MACmed	WPA		Palest pink	FF
Sympathie		WPA		Scarlet	F
Tradition*	KORkeltin	WPA		Crimson	FF
Warm Welcome*	CHEWizz	PA		Orange-vermilion	FF
White Cloud	KORstacha	W		Creamy white	FFF

Colour schemes for roses

There exists a range of popular colour schemes involving roses, co-ordinated and not, and the following lists may be of some help in planning your beds and borders as well as walls, fences and patio containers. The suggestions are not intended as hard and fast rules but simply as a guide to the sort of roses you may choose after deciding on a colour scheme for your garden. They can be used when planning a rose-only bed, to avoid colour clashes – unless this is your intention when planning your garden – and may be used in conjunction with your choice of companion plants (see pages 46–49).

Vermilion and scarlet
Bedding Alexander, Cleopatra, Fellowship, Fragrant Cloud, Trumpeter, St. Boniface, Top Marks
Climbing Danse du Feu, Climbing Orange Sunblaze, Sympathie

Orange and yellow
Bedding Amber Queen, Belle Epoque, Dawn Chorus, Fellowship, Freedom, Irish Eyes, Just Joey, Korresia, Mandarin, Molineux, Peace, Remember Me, Selfridges, Tequila Sunrise
Patio containers Gwent, Irish Eyes, Mandarin
Borders Golden Celebration, Golden Wings, Graham Thomas, Gwent, Molineux, Oranges and Lemons, Peace, Selfridges
Climbing Dreaming Spires, Golden Showers, Golden Celebration, Graham Thomas, Joseph's Coat, Laura Ford, Sunrise, Warm Welcome

Yellow and gold
Bedding Amber Queen, Elina, Freedom, Gwent, Just Joey, Korresia, Molineux, Selfridges
Patio containers Gwent, Worcestershire
Borders Golden Celebration, Golden Wings, Graham Thomas, Molineux, Peace, Selfridges, The Pilgrim, Worcestershire

Climbing Dreaming Spires, Graham Thomas, Golden Celebration, Golden Showers, Laura Ford, The Pilgrim

Apricot and gold
Bedding Belle Epoque, Crystal Palace, Dawn Chorus, Elina, English Garden, Evelyn, Just Joey, Sunset Boulevard, Sweet Dream
Borders Buff Beauty

Peaches and cream
Bedding Crystal Palace, Elina, English Garden, Evelyn, Paul Shirville, Sunset Boulevard, Sweet Dream
Borders English Garden, Evelyn, Sally Holmes
Climbing Penny Lane, Compassion, Schoolgirl

White
Bedding Avon, Elina, Iceberg, Ice Cream, Kent, Tumbling Waters, White Flower Carpet, White Pet
Borders Iceberg, Jacqueline du Pré, Kent, White Flower Carpet, Winchester Cathedral, *R. rugosa* 'Alba'
Patio containers Avon, Kent, Little White Pet, Tumbling Waters, White Flower Carpet
Climbing Little Rambler, Penny Lane, White Cloud, Swan Lake

White and pink
Bedding Anna Livia, Avon, Congratulations, Geoff Hamilton, Hannah Gordon, Iceberg, Many Happy Returns, Playtime, Queen Mother, Silver Jubilee, The Fairy, White Flower Carpet, Winchester Cathedral
Borders Ballerina, Comte de Chambord, Congratulations, Felicia, Geoff Hamilton, Heritage, Playtime, St. Tiggywinkle, Sharifa Asma, Winchester Cathedral, Frau Dagmar Hastrup, *R. rugosa* 'Alba', *R. rugosa* 'Rubra'
Patio containers Avon, Little Bo-Peep, Pink Hit, Queen Mother, The Fairy, White Flower Carpet

Climbing
Climbing Agatha Christie, Bantry Bay, Compassion, Graham Thomas, Handel, Little Rambler, Nice Day, Open Arms, Penny Lane, Swan Lake, New Dawn

Shades of pink
Bedding Anna Livia, Ballerina, Comte de Chambord, Congratulations, Fascination, Flower Carpet, Geoff Hamilton, Hertfordshire, L'Aimant, Many Happy Returns, Mary Rose, Oxfordshire, Playtime, Queen Mother, Silver Jubilee, The Fairy, Wiltshire
Borders Ballerina, Berkshire, Comte de Chambord, Congratulations, Cornelia, Felicia, Flower Carpet, Geoff Hamilton, Gertrude Jekyll, Jacques Cartier, Mary Rose, Oxfordshire, Sharifa Asma, Surrey, The Fairy, Wiltshire, Frau Dagmar Hastrup, *R. rugosa* 'Rubra'
Climbing Agatha Christie, Bantry Bay, Compassion, Nice Day, Open Arms, Summer Wine, New Dawn

Pink and red
Bedding Anne Livia, Berkshire, Congratulations, Flower Carpet, Festival, Ingrid Bergman, Intrigue, L'Aimant, Mary Rose, Royal William, Surrey, The Times, Trumpeter, Wiltshire
Borders Berkshire, Charles Notcutt, Felicia, Cornelia, Kordes' Robusta, Mary Rose, Surrey, Wiltshire
Climbing Agatha Christie, Altissimo, Bantry Bay, Grand Hotel, Sympathie, Tradition

Crimson
Bedding Festival, Ingrid Bergman, Intrigue, Lancashire, Royal William, The Times, Suffolk
Borders Charles Notcutt, L.D. Braithwaite, De Rescht, Kordes' Robusta, Lancashire, Suffolk
Climbing Altissimo, Grand Hotel, Sympathie, Tradition

Useful addresses

Many garden centres stock a fine selection of rose varieties. If they do not have what you want, ask to see a copy of the book called *Find that Rose*, compiled by the British Rose Growers Association, to trace possible sources – there should be a copy at the sales desk. You might even persuade the garden centre to order the variety you are looking for.

The Royal National Rose Society, founded in 1876, is the world's leading specialist plant society, with a flourishing worldwide membership. Besides helping to promote the rose, the Society plays a vital role in conserving an important part of our plant heritage. Find out about the benefits of membership by contacting them at the address below.

The Royal National Rose Society
Chiswell Green, St. Albans,
Herts AL2 3NR
01727 850461
mail@rnrs.org.uk

David Austin Roses Ltd
Bowling Green Lane, Albrighton,
Shropshire WV73 HB
01902 376377

Peter Beales Roses
London Road, Attleborough,
Norfolk NR17 1AY
01953 454707

Burrows Roses
Meadowcroft, Spondon Road, Dale Abbey,
Derby DE74 PQ
01332 668289

Cants of Colchester Ltd
Nayland Road, Mile End, Colchester,
Essex CO4 5EB
01206 84408

James Cocker & Sons
Whitemyres, Lang Stracht,
Aberdeen AB15 2EX
01224 313261

Fryers Nurseries Ltd
Manchester Road, Knutsford,
Cheshire WA16 0SX
01565 755455

Gandy's Roses Ltd
North Kilworth, Lutterworth,
Leics LE16 6HZ
01858 880398

R. Harkness & Co Ltd.
Cambridge Road, Hitchin,
Herts SG4 0JT
01462 420402

C & K Jones
Goldenfields Nursery, Barrow Lane,
Cheshire CH3 8JF
01829 740663

LeGrice Roses
Thorpe Market Road, Roughton, nr Cromer,
Norfolk NR11 8TB
01263 833111

Mattocks Roses
Notcutts Ltd, Woodbridge,
Suffolk IP12 4AP
08457 585652
and various other Notcutts Garden Centres in England

Pocock's Nurseries
Jermyns Lane, Romsey,
Hants SO51 0QA
01794 367500

Rumwood Nurseries
Langley, Maidstone,
Kent ME17 3ND
01622 861477

Scotts Nurseries (Merriott) Ltd
Merriott, Somerset TA16 5PL
01460 72306

Henry Street Nursery
Swallowfield Road, Arborfield, Reading,
Berks RG2 9JY
01189 761223

Index of rose names

Index

Page numbers in italic refer to the illustrations

Author's acknowledgments

Mark Mattock wishes to thank the following:

Mattocks Roses division of Notcutts Nurseries for supplying specimen blooms; Linda Burgess whose personal style of photography ensured that the evocative flower portraits add great originality to this book; Finest English Conservatories whose showhouses at Notcutts Garden Centre at Nuneham Courtenay provided excellent studio facilities for photography; James Mattock and Debbie Godfrey whose expertise on word processing and computers provided admirable support; members of the rose growing confraternity, including Angela Pawsey (editor of *Find that Rose*) and Ken Grapes (Director General of the Royal National Rose Society) whose interest and enthusiasm have encouraged the writing of this book. And, last but by no means least, all at Quadrille who have been involved with seeing the book through from its inception to its production with understanding and kindness.

Picture credits

The publisher thanks the photographers and agencies for their kind permission to reproduce the following photographs in this book:

2 Le Scanff-Mayer (Pépinère Delbard à Malicorne); 6 A Bouquet of Roses by Eugene Henri Cauchois (1850-1911) Private Collection/Bridgeman Art Library; 9 Royal Horticultural Society, Lindley Library; 10 Adelia aurclianensis, engraved by Victor, from 'Choix des Plus Belles Fleurs', 1827 (coloured engraving) by Pierre Joseph Redoute (1759-1840) (after) Private Collection/Bridgeman Art Library; 12 Royal Horticultural Society, Lindley Library; 15 The Art Archive/Victoria & Albert Museum, London; 18 Simon McBride/Interior Archive (Garden: Jan Morgan); 20 Jerry Harpur (Designer: Diana Ross, London); 21 Jerry Harpur (Designer: Lisette Pleasance, London); 22 left Saxon Holt; 22-23 centre Simon McBride/Interior Archive (Garden: Hawkes); 23 above right John Glover; 24 left Andrew Lawson; 24-5 Andrew Lawson (Designer: Penelope Hobhouse); 26 left Nicola Browne (Designer: Gilles Clement); 26-27 Brigitte Thomas/GPL; 28 left Marcus Harpur (The Vine, Essex); 28 right Clive Nichols (Designer: Roger Platts); 29 Andrew Lawson (Designer: Wendy Lauderdale); 30 Le Scanff-Mayer (Le Jardin d'Anne-Marie (91) Lardy, France); 31 John Glover; 32 left Nicola Browne; 32 right Densey Clyne/GPL; 33 Clive Nichols (Meadow Plants, Berks); 34 left John Glover; 34-35 Ron Sutherland/GPL; 36 Jerry Harpur (Designer: Diana Ross, London); 37 Saxon Holt; 38 Clive Nichols (Designer: Sarah Raven – Daily Telegraph/American Express Garden, Chelsea Flower Show 1998); 39 Clive Nichols (Lower Hall, Shrops); 40 Marcus Harpur (Designer: Penelope Hobhouse); 41 Andrew Lawson; 42-43 Jerry Harpur (Designers: Janowski & Tokstad, San Francisco, CA); 44 Andrew Lawson (Designer: Penelope Hobhouse); 45 John Glover (Chelsea Flower Show, 1994); 46-7 Dency Kane (Designer: Brooks Garcia); 48 John Glover (Parham Park); 49 above Le Scanff-Mayer (Pépinère Delbard à Malicorne); 49 below Karen Bussolini; 148-149 Simon McBride/Interior Archive (Garden: Jan Morgan); 152-3 S&O Mathews; 156-7 S&O Mathews; 158 Le Scanff-Mayer (Jardin de Guy Thenot);

All other photographs were specially taken by Linda Burgess for Quadrille Publishing Limited.